NATIONAL STUDIES ON INTERNATIONAL ORGANIZATION

# JAPAN
## AND THE
# UNITED NATIONS

Report of a Study Group
set up by the
Japanese Association of International Law

Prepared for the
CARNEGIE ENDOWMENT FOR INTERNATIONAL PEACE

GREENWOOD PRESS, PUBLISHERS
WESTPORT, CONNECTICUT

**Library of Congress Cataloging in Publication Data**

Kokusaihō Gakkai.
Japan and the United Nations.

Reprint of the 1958 ed. published by Manhattan Pub. Co., New York, in series: National studies on international organization.
Includes bibliographical references.
1. United Nations--Japan. I. Carnegie Endowment for International Peace. II. Title. III. Series: National studies on international organization.
[JX1977.2.J3K6 1974] 341.23'52 74-7433
ISBN 0-8371-7538-0

Originally published in 1958 by Manhattan Publishing Company, New York

Reprinted with the permission of Manhattan Publishing Company

Reprinted in 1974 by Greenwood Press,
a division of Williamhouse-Regency Inc.

Library of Congress Catalog Card Number 74-7433

ISBN 0-8371-7538-0

Printed in the United States of America

# Preface

This volume forms part of a series of studies on international organization initiated by the Carnegie Endowment for International Peace and carried out by private institutions and individuals in more than twenty countries around the world. This particular study was prepared by Professor Kisaburo Yokota and the late Professor Tomoo Otaka, under the auspices of the Japanese Association of International Law.

The decision, taken in 1952, to initiate this program reflected both the Endowment's long-standing conviction that international organizations, such as the United Nations, are central to the quest for peace and the assumption that their significance and functioning depend first and foremost upon the attitudes and policies of nations. The fact that the question of Charter review would be on the agenda of the General Assembly in 1955 seemed to afford a unique opportunity for assessing the strengths and weaknesses of the United Nations in terms of national expectations and their fulfillment during the brief but rich testing period of the first ten years. In sponsoring this series of studies the Endowment has sought to encourage an exchange of unofficial national views, with the object of stimulating a closer examination of the past record and future potentialities of the United Nations and of increasing understanding of differences and similarities in national attitudes toward the Organization.

In the pursuit of these objectives, the participants in each country were asked to appraise their national experience with international organization, especially the United Nations. In doing so they have considered such questions as: What impact has the United Nations had on both the content and the conduct of national policy? To what extent have the purposes and principles set out in the Charter served as adequate guides to the organs of the United Nations in their operations? Have developments in the practices and the procedures of the United Nations made the organization more or less effective as an agency to achieve the purposes for which it was established? What is, and should be, the relationship of the United Nations to other forms of international organization, including regional systems? Does experience suggest the need for formal revision of the Charter?

Japan has only recently become a member of the United Nations; but, as this study shows, the Japanese people have been deeply interested in the Organization ever since the end of the Second World War. Although Japan was for many years frustrated in its desire to join the United Nations, the government, the political parties, the press, and scholarly and intellectual circles continually expressed their concern with the effectiveness of the United Nations system and the ways in which it could be strengthened.

These studies have been undertaken on the initiative of the Carnegie Endowment for International Peace. However, they have been carried out independently of that organization and the responsibility for the contents of the individual volumes, therefore, lies with the authors.

In exercising its responsibility for the decision to publish the volumes in this series, the Endowment has been assisted by an advisory review committee, comprising Dr. Alberto Lleras Camargo, former President of Colombia and former Secretary General of the Organization of American States; Sir Ramaswami Mudaliar, Vice-Chancellor of Travancore University, India; and Dr. Bernard H. M. Vlekke, Secretary-General of the Netherlands Institute of International Affairs. Their faithful and wise counsel is most gratefully acknowledged.

The conclusions of the individual studies will be summarized and their significance analyzed in two final volumes prepared independently by Robert MacIver, Lieber Professor Emeritus of Political Philosophy and Sociology at Columbia University; and Maurice Bourquin, Professor of International Public Law at the University of Geneva.

No prefatory note which did not exceed its proper dimensions could possibly acknowledge all the debts which the Endowment owes to scholars and officials in many parts of the world for the help which they have graciously given. To the Japanese Association of International Law, and especially to Professor Kisaburo Yokota, its President, particular thanks are due for their co-operation in making the present volume possible. The Endowment wishes to record its deep appreciation not only for the scholarship and thought which are reflected in the following pages but also for the patience and unfailing courtesy they have shown in this venture in co-operation over several years.

The Endowment wishes to express its gratitude to the Ford Foundation for providing a grant which, by supplementing funds supplied by the Endowment and the co-operating institutions themselves, made it possible to carry out the project on a broad and comprehensive basis.

October 1957

JOSEPH E. JOHNSON
*President*
Carnegie Endowment for International Peace

## VOLUMES PREVIOUSLY PUBLISHED IN THIS SERIES

LA BELGIQUE ET LES NATIONS UNIES, prepared under the auspices of the Institut Royal des Relations Internationales

BRITAIN AND THE UNITED NATIONS, prepared under the auspices of the Royal Institute of International Affairs

CANADA AND THE UNITED NATIONS, prepared under the auspices of the Canadian Institute of International Affairs

DENMARK AND THE UNITED NATIONS, by Max Sørensen and Niels J. Haagerup

EGYPT AND THE UNITED NATIONS, by a Special Study Group of the Egyptian Society of International Law

LA GRECE ET LES NATIONS UNIES, prepared under the auspices of the Société d'Etudes Internationales d'Athènes

INDIA AND THE UNITED NATIONS, by a Special Study Group of the Indian Council of World Affairs

ISRAEL AND THE UNITED NATIONS, by a Special Study Group of the Hebrew University of Jerusalem

LA SUISSE ET LES NATIONS UNIES, by Jacqueline Belin

SWEDEN AND THE UNITED NATIONS, by a Special Study Group of the Swedish Institute of International Affairs

PRINTED BY BRÜDER ROSENBAUM, VIENNA (AUSTRIA)

# Foreword

At the request of the Carnegie Endowment for International Peace, the Japanese Association of International Law undertook in February 1953 the responsibility for carrying out a study of the national policy and public attitude of Japan toward international organizations, with particular emphasis on the United Nations. The Association set up a small committee to work out a plan of research on the basis of suggestions by the Carnegie Endowment. The members of this committee were: Mr. Hidebumi Egawa, Professor of Private International Law, Tokyo University; Mr. Zengo Ohira, Professor of International Law, Hitotsubashi University; Mr. Kisaburo Yokota, Emeritus Professor of Tokyo University, President of Japanese Association of International Law, Member of International Law Commission of the United Nations; and the late Mr. Tomoo Otaka, who at the time of his death in May 1956 was Professor of Jurisprudence, Tokyo University.

The initial research work was carried out by the following scholars, each responsible for a special subject:

National Policy toward the United Nations (consisting mainly of an analysis of the discussion on the United Nations in the Diet)
Mr. Naoki Kobayashi, Assistant Professor of Jurisprudence, Tokyo University

Public Attitude toward the United Nations (the discussions on the United Nations in the leading newspapers and magazines)
Mr. Shigeru Inoue, Assistant Professor of Jurisprudence, Ochanomizu University

Purpose and Principles of the United Nations
Mr. Yasuo Yamashita, Professor of International Law, Nagoya University

The Principle of Domestic Jurisdiction
Mr. Masao Ichimata, Professor of International Law, Waseda University

Membership in the United Nations
Mr. Ryoichi Taoka, Professor of International Law, Kyoto University and Mr. Yuichi Takano, Professor of International Law, Tokyo University

The Maintenance of Peace and Security
Mr. Mitsuo Maehara, Professor of International Law, Keio University

Economic and Social Problems
Mr. Zengo Ohira, Professor of International Law, Hitotsubashi University

Influence of Important Events since 1945
Mr. Keishiro Irie, Professor of International Law, Aichi University

In order to get the opinions of well-informed people, a detailed questionnaire was sent to scholars, journalists, ex-diplomats, and other intellectuals. The questionnaire set forth the objective of the study and, since it was recognized that the people whose views were sought might not possess detailed knowledge of the problems in question, the questionnaire was accompanied by concise explanations.

Professor K. Yokota and Professor T. Otaka then summarized and arranged these two series of data—the initial research reports by the professors and the answers to the questionnaire—so that they might constitute a basis for discussion by a special study group established in accordance with the suggestions of the Carnegie Endowment. The task of this group, which consisted of persons specially qualified by reason of knowledge and experience in the field of international relations, was to consider the initial research reports from a broad point of view, to exchange opinions on the matters treated therein, and, insofar as possible, to reach constructive conclusions. The Study Group met nine times between 5 December 1953 and 9 March 1954. These meetings were chaired, in turn, by Professor Yokota and Professor Otaka. The other members of this group were:

| | |
|---|---|
| Mr. Naotake Sato | President of the United Nations Association of Japan; member of the Diet; former Ambassador to Belgium, France, and Russia; former Minister for Foreign Affairs |
| Mr. Tamon Maeda | President of the National Commission for UNESCO; former Minister of Education; former Representative of Japan at the International Labour Organisation |
| Mr. Shigeharu Matsumoto | Managing Director of the International House of Japan; former Chief Editor of the Domei News Agency of Japan |
| Mr. Shintaro Ryu | Editor-in-Chief of the newspaper *Asahi* |
| Mr. Fumio Ikematsu | Editor-in-Chief of the newspaper *Mainichi* |
| Mr. Masamichi Royama | President of Ochanomizu University; former Professor of Political Science, Tokyo University |

| | |
|---|---|
| Mr. Ichiro Nakayama | Professor of Economics, former President, Hitotsubashi University; Governmental Representative to the Conference of the International Labour Organisation in 1953 and 1954 |
| Miss Taki Fujita | Professor of Tsudajyuku University; former Director of the Women's and Minors' Bureau, Ministry of Labor |
| Mr. Yuhiko Hamaguchi | President of the Tokyo Bank; Director of the United Nations Association of Japan |
| Mr. Eiji Amau | Vice-President of the United Nations Association of Japan; former Ambassador to Italy; former Vice-Minister for Foreign Affairs |
| Mr. Tetsuzo Tanikawa | Dean of the Faculty of Literature, Hosei University |
| Miss Shio Sakanishi | Writer; former Technical Advisor to the Foreign Affairs Committee, House of Councillors |

To supplement the discussions and opinions of the Study Group, a series of special meetings were held. The first was a meeting with the Japan Federation of Economic Organizations, the most influential business group in Japan. The expectations of Japanese economic and financial circles concerning the United Nations were discussed and frank opinions were expressed, especially regarding the economic activities of the United Nations. A second meeting, to hear the opinions of personnel in the Foreign Ministry, was attended by more than fifteen officials. Opinions were freely given in order that attitudes toward the United Nations in government circles might be known. This was not the official view of the government, but was the basis of it. A great deal was learned from this meeting. Thirdly, meetings were held in cities other than Tokyo (in Osaka, Kyoto, and Hiroshima), which were attended by scholars, financial people, and representatives of the various women's organizations.

These discussions were then summed up by Professor Yokota and Professor Otaka. Recognizing that their efforts to present the material in an objective manner may not have been completely successful, the two authors assumed the responsibility for the final report embodying the results of the research and discussions.

The study itself is divided in three parts. Part One traces the development of Japanese attitudes concerning the United Nations from the end of the war to the beginning of 1953. It is based on a detailed analysis of the discussions in the Japanese Diet and the Japanese press. The organization and functioning of the United Nations system, and Japanese views on various problems involved, are examined in Part Two. Part Three discusses the concern of the United Nations with Far Eastern problems and the role of the Organization in relation to Japan's security. The concluding chapter recounts Japan's efforts to gain admission to the United Nations and its objectives in joining the Organization.

The Japanese Association of International Law would like to take this opportunity to thank the members of the Study Group, the scholars who engaged in the research, and the people who sent in their replies to the questionnaire. Thanks are also due to Mr. Shigeharu Matsumoto, Managing Director of the International House of Japan, who most generously undertook to arrange for the meetings held in Tokyo as well as for the English translation of this report and numerous other details connected with this project.

It is appropriate to conclude this note with a tribute to the contribution of Professor Tomoo Otaka, whose death in May 1956 was a source of deep regret. From the very beginning of the project, he collaborated wholeheartedly with Professor Yokota and others in working out the scheme of research, putting it into execution, and drafting the final report. It is a thousand pities that he died shortly after the completion of the work and left it to Professor Yokota alone to sign this *Foreword.*

July 1957

KISABURO YOKOTA
*President*
Japanese Association of International Law

# Contents

# DEVELOPMENT OF JAPAN'S ATTITUDE TOWARD THE UNITED NATIONS

## PART ONE

*chapter one*

# Introduction

There is no doubt that throughout the years since the end of the Second World War the large majority of the Japanese people have been sympathetically inclined toward the ideals of the Charter of the United Nations. Great hopes were entertained that this new international peace organization would prove to be a distinct improvement over the League of Nations. As a nation that had known the terrors of a war which was one of its own making, and particularly as the world's first actual victim of atomic disaster, it was only natural that Japan should have wholeheartedly sought an end to all wars. Under the Allied occupation Japan not only cast off the remnants of its huge armaments but also placed a voluntary ban upon military preparations of all sorts. A formal declaration renouncing war was incorporated in Article 9 of the new Constitution enacted on 3 November 1946. It was inevitable that the Japanese people, having discarded ultra-militarism and having adopted a constitution calling for absolute pacifism of a kind unprecedented in the history of mankind, should have had much in common with both the ideals and spirit of the United Nations Charter and should have looked to that Organization for the maintenance of their own security.

## TREND OF PUBLIC OPINION

In analyzing the attitudes of the Japanese government, political parties, and the general public toward the United Nations, it is appropriate to divide the postwar era into four periods, each of which will be examined in detail in the following chapters. During the first period, from the early stage of the occupation to the end of 1948, the Japanese people, deprived of political autonomy, sympathized with the ideals of the United Nations and apprehensively watched it face difficult problems. In the second period, from the beginning of 1949 to June 1950, an attitude of strong neutralism was observable in public opinion, instigated by General MacArthur's statement that Japan should become "the Switzerland of the Pacific." The rise of neutralism to a certain extent paralleled increasing misgivings concerning the United Nations. In the face of the intense reality of the international political situation during the third period (from June 1950, when the Korean War broke out, to February 1951), neutralism declined and at the same time attitudes favoring the United Nations increased. During the fourth period the Peace Treaty and the Security Treaty between Japan and the United States were concluded. Following the conclusion of the treaties in September 1951, Japan applied for admission to membership in the United Nations. This application was supported by majorities in both the Security Council and the General Assembly of the United Nations but was blocked by Soviet opposition. Thus at the end of 1952 Japan had still not achieved its goal of becoming a member of the United Nations.[1] Japan had, however, become a

[1] While Part One of this study covers only the period from 1945 to the beginning of 1953, the subsequent successful effort of Japan to gain admission to the United Nations is described in Part Three. See below, Chapter 12.

member of the specialized agencies of the United Nations and, through these channels, was earnestly co-operating with the United Nations.

The trend of public opinion toward the United Nations, as reflected in the leading newspapers and magazines in Japan, has followed approximately the same course as attitudes in political circles. The principal difference has been that the government and the political parties have dealt mainly with the immediate political problems facing Japan, particularly security problems; the newspapers and magazines, on the other hand, have considered the United Nations from a wider perspective and their observations and arguments have been more objective. They have dealt with the ideals of the United Nations, the difficulties the Organization has faced, and the defects in the structure of the United Nations itself.

## ATTITUDES OF POLITICAL PARTIES

Throughout the postwar period most political parties consistently held the view that the security of a disarmed Japan could only be maintained through the United Nations and that admission to the Organization should be ardently sought. The Communist party, despite its initial strong support for the United Nations and for Japan's participation therein, began to heap open abuse upon the Organization after the outbreak of the Korean War. This was done on the pretense that the United Nations had deteriorated into a mere tool of United States policy. Moreover, in the leftist faction of the Socialist party, which professed itself to be distinguishable from the Communist party, there were some who looked upon the United Nations with a critical eye. They regarded it as an arena of controversies in power politics and asserted that Japan's participation in it would, under the circumstances, be undesirable.

There were also some doubts whether membership in the United Nations, with its obligations concerning military sanctions against aggression, would be compatible with the position of a nation that sought to stand outside international conflicts and follow a policy of neutrality.[2] Because of this, vacillation regarding the desirability of joining the United Nations developed among the more progressive parties, which strongly supported the stand of permanent neutrality for Japan. The question was raised whether Japan's admission to the United Nations might not entail responsibilities for participating in military sanctions when the need arose. Those favoring Japan's permanent disarmament were of the opinion that, in the event of admission, Japan should make reservations for the time being regarding such responsibilities. On the other hand, the Liberal party, which was in power for most of the postwar period, and other parties holding similar conservative and anti-Communist views maintained a definite attitude in favor of co-operating with the United Nations. This was especially true after opposition between the free nations and the Communist bloc culminated in the outbreak of the Korean War. As an intermediary step to admission to the United Nations, they sought the maintenance of Japanese security through the assistance of specific nations. The first fruits of this policy were manifest in the agreements reached at the Peace Conference held in San Francisco in 1951.

## POSTWAR POLITICS

Before proceeding to a detailed analysis of Japanese attitudes toward the United Nations, it may be useful to examine briefly the political composition of the Cabinet and the Diet, noting the major changes which took place in the period from the end of the war to 1953.

The interim cabinet headed by Prince Naruhiko Higashikuni, which was formed immediately after the end of the war to administer a devastated country, resigned *en masse* on 5 October 1945. The

[2] This issue of the compatibility of neutrality and membership in the United Nations and the related issue of Japan's security are discussed at some length in Part Three of this study. See below, Chapter 11.

Shidehara Cabinet which followed possessed strong conservative tendencies. However, at the suggestion of the headquarters of the Supreme Commander for the Allied Powers, the Cabinet brought forth a draft plan for a new Constitution. As compared with the previous Constitution of the Meiji era, this was a revolutionary document. In April 1946 a general election for the House of Representatives was held under the new election law. The result was that the Liberal party (conservative) came to power with 141 seats. The Progressive party (also a conservative party, despite its name) became the second party with 93 seats; the Socialist party followed with 92 seats, and the Communist party with five. The first Yoshida Cabinet of the Liberal party, formed on 22 May, was based on this new party distribution.

The Yoshida Cabinet took over the draft plan of the new Constitution from the Shidehara Cabinet and presented it to the Imperial Diet, which was still functioning under the old Meiji Constitution. The Diet deliberated on it during the long session lasting from June to October 1946. The new Constitution was promulgated on 3 November 1946 and went into effect on 3 May 1947. Under its terms the Emperor, who had hitherto supposedly governed Japan according to divine will, was now removed from actual political power. He became a symbol of the state but sovereignty was declared to reside in the people. At the same time, according to Article 9 of the new Constitution, Japan forsook all armaments, renounced the right of belligerency, and became a nation entirely without defense. As a result, Japan, far more than any other nation, became unavoidably dependent for its security upon the United Nations. An important issue developed whether or not Japan could remain a completely defenseless nation and still sometime in the future become a responsible member of the United Nations security system.

The first general election under the new Constitution took place in April 1947. The outcome was that the Socialist party made large gains and became the first party in both Houses of the new National Diet. The Liberal party became the second party and the Democratic party (formerly the Progressive party) followed. The strength of the political parties was as follows:

| | Lower House (House of Representatives) | Upper House (House of Councillors) |
|---|---|---|
| Socialist party | 143 | 46 |
| Liberal party | 131 | 40 |
| Democratic party | 124 | 30 |
| People's Co-operative party | 31 | 9 |
| Communist party | 4 | 5 |
| Small parties group | 20 | 10 |
| Independent | 13 | 110 |
| Total | 466 | 250 |

The Katayama Cabinet was then formed by the Socialist party but the political situation remained unstable. The Katayama Cabinet resigned in February 1948 and a new Cabinet under Mr. Hitoshi Ashida of the Democratic party followed. However, the Ashida Cabinet was also short-lived and it resigned in October 1948. The Liberal party came into power and the Second Yoshida Cabinet was formed.

In January 1949, when the second general election of the Lower House took place, the Liberal party won overwhelmingly, getting a clear majority. At the same time, the Communist party showed a great gain, while the influence of the Socialist party waned. The distribution of seats was as follows:

| | Lower House |
|---|---|
| Liberal party | 264 |
| Democratic party | 68 |
| Socialist party | 49 |
| Communist party | 35 |
| People's Co-operative party | 14 |
| Workers and Farmers party | 7 |
| Small parties group | 17 |
| Independent | 12 |
| Total | 466 |

In June 1950 the Korean conflict broke out, and Japan became decisively linked to the free world. At the same time, definite preparations were under way for a peace treaty. On 8 September 1951 the Peace Treaty was concluded in San Francisco and at the same time the Security Treaty between Japan and the United States, which was to ensure the defense of Japan, was signed. At this point a struggle developed within the Socialist party between the right wing, which opposed the Security Treaty but supported the Peace Treaty, and the left wing, which opposed both treaties. As a result, the Socialist party finally broke in two. On 28 April 1952 the Peace Treaty came into effect, the occupation of Japan by the Allied forces came to an end, and Japan resumed its position as a full-fledged member of the international community.

In August of the same year the government, acting under the provisions of Article 7 of the Constitution, dissolved the Lower House and in October the third general election was carried out. Although the Liberal party's strength decreased slightly, the Communist party did not get even a single seat. The Democratic party, resuming the name Progressive party, became the second party in the conservative camp, and proceeded to advocate a program of rearmament.

| | Lower House |
|---|---|
| Liberal party | 240 |
| Progressive party | 85 |
| Right Wing Socialist party | 57 |
| Left Wing Socialist party | 54 |
| Workers and Farmers party | 4 |
| Small parties group | 7 |
| Independent | 19 |
| Total | 466 |

Thus, at the beginning of 1953, the Liberal party was still in power, although its position was becoming increasingly shaky.[3]

[3] After the 1952 election, the strength of the Liberal party declined and it ceased to command a majority of seats in the House of Representatives. At the same

In order to give a more accurate picture of the main trends of opinion in Japan with regard to the United Nations during each of the four periods mentioned above, the official views of the government and the political parties, and the general tendencies of opinion in non-governmental circles have been treated separately in the following four chapters.

There are two kinds of material available for this analysis. The first is the discussions by representatives of the government, major political parties, and others in the Diet.[4] The second consists of reviews on the United Nations that have appeared in leading newspapers and magazines.[5] For this study, three outstanding newspapers, *Asahi*, *Mainichi*, and *Yomiuri*, have been selected. The political attitudes of these newspapers vary from time to time, but generally speaking, *Asahi* is more or less progressive, *Yomiuri* is comparatively conservative, and *Mainichi* is in between. Three representative magazines have also been singled out for analysis: *Sekai* (World), *Chuo-Koron* (Central Review), and *Kaizo* (Recon-

---

time both wings of the Socialist party increased their strength. In the spring of 1953, a group of Liberals, led by Ichiro Hatoyama, refused to support Yoshida; through their abstentions on a vote of confidence, the government fell. During the April elections the Hatoyama group won 34 seats in the House of Representatives; the Right and Left Wing Socialist parties gained strength; but Yoshida still commanded sufficient support within the Liberal and Progressive parties to form a new government.

When Yoshida resigned in December 1954, he was succeeded by Hatoyama, whose party, the Japan-Democrats, won a plurality, though not a majority, in the subsequent election of February 1955. In this election the Right and Left Wing Socialist parties made further gains and, when the two wings united in October 1955, their combined strength in the Diet almost equalled that of the Japan-Democrats. At this point the Democrats merged with the Liberals to form the Liberal-Democratic party. After Hatoyama's resignation in December 1956, the coalition continued under Tanzan Ishibashi, who in turn was succeeded in February 1957 by Nobusuke Kishi.

[4] The proceedings of the Diet are published in the *Official Gazette Extra*. Throughout this study, quotations from Diet debates for the period May 1946 to April 1952 are from the official English language edition of this publication. Quotations from subsequent Diet debates and from discussions in the foreign affairs committees are translations by the authors.

All quotations from Japanese newspapers and magazines are translations by the authors.

struction). The tendency of these magazines is progressive as compared with the above newspapers; *Sekai* and *Kaizo* sometimes contain radical articles. As far as the arguments on the United Nations are concerned, however, the political color of these magazines is of little consequence. The purpose of the following four chapters is to describe as objectively as possible, on the basis of the above-mentioned materials, the changes in public attitudes and evaluations in Japan with respect to the United Nations.

*chapter two*

# The First Period: Occupation

(September 1945—December 1948)

Before the Japanese people had been able to grasp the exact meaning of the serious situation brought about by atom-bombing on 6 and 9 August 1945, they were informed at noon on 15 August by the Emperor's speech (delivered for the first time over the radio) that the fierce war had been brought to an end by Japan's acceptance of the Potsdam Declaration. For some time after that, the greatest concern of the Japanese was to support themselves and to save their families from hunger. Most cities were in ruins; the food-producing capacity of agricultural villages had been hard hit; and all economic functions were in a state of paralysis. What was still worse, the people were left without spiritual support. The mode of living at that time has been described as "a state of absent-mindedness." The most urgent problems faced by the government and the Diet were maintaining a minimum living standard and re-establishing internal order.

## THE NEW CONSTITUTION OF JAPAN

The first step toward the construction of a new Japan was the enactment of the new Constitution. When the 90th Session of the Imperial Diet opened in June 1946, it received from the Cabinet the amending bill which, in fact, had been secretly prepared by the headquarters of the Supreme Commander for the Allied Powers. Although the amendment was carried out under the guise of constitutional revision in accordance with Article 73 of the Meiji Constitution, this virtually implied the establishment of a new Constitution for the basic democratization of the national life of Japan. It is not, therefore, surprising that the major provisions of the bill, should have provoked serious arguments, despite the dampened spirits of the people in the early stages of the occupation.

As was to be expected, lively debate centered on Article 9 of the bill, which provided for the renunciation of war as a sovereign right of the nation. It read as follows:

> Aspiring sincerely to an international peace based on justice and order, the Japanese people forever renounce war as a sovereign right of the nation and the threat or use of force as means of settling international disputes.
>
> In order to accomplish the aim of the preceding paragraph, land, sea, and air forces, as well as other war potential, will never be maintained. The right of belligerency of the state will not be recognized.

This declaration of ultrapacifism, unparalleled in the history of mankind, was impressed upon the minds of the Japanese, who had just awakened from the nightmare of war, as the manifestation of a lofty ideal. At the same time it aroused grave doubts regarding Japan's ability, as a totally disarmed nation, to maintain its own security. The first mention of the United Nations in the Diet deliberations was in connection with Japan's security, the question upon which all discussions concerning Article 9 were focussed.

The Cabinet under Prime Minister Yoshida, as sponsor of the bill, was naturally of the opinion that the expression of absolute pacifism in Article 9 should be left unchanged. With regard to the relation between Article 9 and the right of self-defense, Prime Minister Yoshida was confident that there would be no need to exercise this right if an international peace organization were set up. At the plenary session of the House of Representatives on 28 June 1946, he replied as follows to Sanzo Nozaka, a leading Communist, who wanted to differentiate between denouncing a "war of invasion" and upholding the right of a "war for self-defence":

> The proposition to recognize the legitimacy of a war . . . made by way of exercising the right of self-defense of a State, is a harmful idea, involving, as it does, the provocation of war. . . . The very idea of recognizing the right of legitimate self-defense, in the event that an international peace organization has been established, is in itself harmful.[1]

This position was unacceptable to the opposition parties, which either remained sceptical as to Article 9 or asserted that Japan, as an independent state, needed armaments for self-defense. It is of considerable significance that within a few years, these early positions were reversed. Those who had once been most emphatic about the necessity of armaments apostatized therefrom and adopted a position of absolute pacifism while at the same time the Yoshida Cabinet, supported by the Liberal party, gradually came to embrace the cause of self-defense, even to the point of supporting rearmament.

A country without arms is not capable of exercising the right of self-defense. Even if such a country nominally possesses the right of self-defense, it is meaningless. The only conceivable alternative was, therefore, for Japan's security to be maintained by recourse to the United Nations. For this reason, the question of admission to the Organization took precedence over all others for Japan. It

[1] Japan, Imperial Diet, *Official Gazette Extra* (English edition), *Minutes of Proceedings in the House of Representatives*, 90th Sess., No. 8, 28 June 1946, p. 15.

may well be said that such was the feeling harbored by a majority of people when Japan's future was considered in relation to Article 9 of the proposed Constitution. Yoshio Suzuki, speaking on behalf of the Socialist party, said:

> It is a matter of course that the proposed renunciation of war does deny the existence of the right of self-defence recognized by international law. We expect, therefore, that when our country is fortunate enough to be permitted to join the United Nations we may be able to ask the said organ for security.[2]

A contrasting view was presented by Kenzo Takayanagi (then Professor of English and American Law at the University of Tokyo and one of the group of scholars who were especially appointed members of the House of Peers in order to engage in the deliberations on constitutional revision). Professor Takayanagi maintained that the establishment of a world federation was long overdue and that the United Nations was but an embryo of this development. In his words, "Article 9 is reasonable on the hypothesis that such a state of human society comes in being."[3] In his view, an international community composed of a number of armed nations was fraught with constant danger of explosion, despite whatever treaties might be concluded among its constituents for the maintenance of peace. A group of nations, all unarmed, would use reason rather than force for the settlement of international disputes. Armed force would be justifiable only when used by the police force of the world federation. He considered that the United Nations had in it the seeds for the establishment of such a federation. How the Organization would develop was a question for the future. But if Article 9 were to be adopted, Japan would find itself under the imperative necessity of requesting speedy admission to the United Nations, thereby assuring its security and helping to establish a

[2] *Ibid.*, No. 6, 26 June 1946, p. 15.

[3] Japan, Imperial Diet, *Official Gazette Extra* (English edition), *Minutes of Proceedings in the House of Peers*, 90th Sess., No. 23, 26 Aug. 1946, pp. 4-5.

world federation. Takayanagi's advocacy of world federation was highly idealistic, but, viewed from another angle, it was based upon a remarkably realistic recognition that unless there was a total renunciation of arms on the part of all nations, Article 9 providing for disarmament of Japan alone was without validity.

Public attention was arrested by Shigeru Nambara (then President of the University of Tokyo, whose specialty was the history of political theory, and who was also a special member of the House of Peers). He was opposed to Article 9 on the ground that in anticipation of Japan's future participation in the United Nations, and in view of the nature of that Organization, Japan would have to provide itself with a minimum of armaments essential to self-defense. His view was roughly as follows: The Charter of the United Nations sanctions the right of self-defense for each of its constituent states. The United Nations has no military organization of its own; it is dependent upon the armed forces that all members are obligated to place at its disposal. He raised the question whether, in the event of admission to the United Nations in the future, Japan intended to give up those rights and duties expressly provided for in the Charter. Will Japan deem it right to abandon itself to the good will and sincerity of foreign nations forever? Should not Japan pursue a positive ideal and share willingly with other nations in the sacrifice of blood and sweat for the cause of liberty and justice for mankind and for the establishing of lasting peace in the world?[4] However, soon afterward Nambara abandoned these views and became strongly antagonistic to rearmament.

The government's answers to these interpellations can be summarized as follows: First, Prime Minister Yoshida stated that he was in general agreement with the view that, if the principle of renunciation of war expressed in Article 9 of the Constitution were adopted, everything must be done to bring about Japan's admission to the United Nations at an early date. However, in view of the

---

[4] *Ibid.*, No. 24, 27 Aug. 1946, pp. 6-7.

restraints placed upon the activities of the Japanese government by the Potsdam Declaration, the question of admission to the United Nations had inevitably to be reserved for the future.[5] With regard to Nosaka's arguments in support of the right of self-defense, Yoshida made it clear that Article 9 should be understood to imply the virtual waiving of the right of self-defense.

Nambara's speech in support of rearmament was also answered by Baron Kijuro Shidehara, Minister of State, who warned:

> Any attempt under the present circumstances to rationalize or legalize some armed sanction as a principle determining . . . international relations is nothing other than a repetition of the numerous failures in the past. . . .
>
> Unless civilization extirpate[s] war quickly, war will extirpate mankind . . . first.[6]

It is worthy of note that these statements by responsible members of the Cabinet did not support the principle of military sanctions as adopted by the United Nations. Premier Yoshida, however, gave no answer concerning the problem of Japan's admission to the United Nations and its position regarding wars of self-defense. He merely stated that:

> the first and most important thing we are required to do . . . is to restore our national rights and independence. The Government is now devoting its time and efforts for the attainment of this important object. . . .[7]

The government's point of view was also clarified by Hitoshi Ashida and Yoshinari Abe, who were the chairmen of the Special Committees for constitutional revision in each house of the Diet. The former reported:

> The view of the Government was that the first Paragraph of Article 9 does not repudiate a war which is for the purpose

[5] *Ibid.*, p. 12.
[6] *Ibid.*, p. 11.
[7] *Ibid.*, p. 12.

> of self-defense, but that the right of belligerency even in that eventuality is denied under the second Paragraph.[8]

On the other hand, Abe stated in the House of Peers that as a result of the total abolition of military force and the negation of the right of war, Japan would find it impracticable to exercise the right of self-defense and therefore would not be in a position to conclude any offensive or defensive alliances with foreign countries. When Japan joined the United Nations, it would be necessary to exempt Japan from the responsibility of providing armed forces. Provisions in the Charter on wars for self-defense and joint defense could not be applied to Japan. He concluded, "In short, the renunciation of war and the repudiation of war potentials and . . . belligerency rights . . . are a mark of our firm determination. [We are] risking our national existence in the hope of saving ourselves."[9]

The government's point of view can be summed up as follows: the security of Japan in the future would be possible only through the strength of the United Nations but the provisions of Article 9 of the Constitution, disapproving any attempt to put the right of self-defense in operation, would preclude Japan from accepting any obligation to provide a military force even in the event that Japan became a member of the United Nations.

The new Constitution, adopted by the Diet on 3 November 1946, took effect on 3 May the following year. In the meantime, the 91st and 92nd Sessions of the Imperial Diet were held and, by the end of 1948, four sessions of the National Diet were convoked under the new Constitution. The Diet, however, was busily occupied with various problems relating to the drastic domestic reforms effected under the occupation; the United Nations was therefore scarcely discussed. This was partly due to the fact that Japan under the occupation was clearly not in a position to meet the conditions for admission to the United Nations. Despite the lack

[8] *Proceedings in the House of Representatives, op. cit.*, No. 35, 24 Aug. 1946, p. 4.
[9] *Proceedings in the House of Peers, op. cit.*, No. 39, 5 Oct. 1946, p. 6.

of discussions on the United Nations in the Diet, there were rising cries for participation in the Organization. For instance, Takeo Miki of the People's Co-operative party stated in the 4th Session of the Diet in 1948:

> . . . The Japanese people . . . hope they will be permitted to join the United Nations as soon as possible, so as to have an opportunity to give expression to their national determination for peaceful construction in the world.

To this, Yoshida replied,

> An early peace-treaty and participation in the United Nations are what [we] are most eagerly looking forward to . . . and of course the Government earnestly hopes for such occasion.[10]

As a background to these views, there was a gloomy anxiety resulting from the opposition between the two worlds with its threatening implications. The belief that feelings of unrest in Japan could be relieved through admission to the United Nations was countered by concern that participation in the Organization might not be consistent with the position of neutralism strongly advocated by the political parties out of power. This problem proved to be the focus of discussion in the Diet during the period discussed in the next chapter.

## VIEWS EXPRESSED IN THE PRESS: 1945-46

Views of the United Nations, as expressed in the Japanese press, during the first year after the end of the war may be roughly classified into two types.

Firstly, severe self-criticism of the militaristic Japan of the past was considered necessary. With an eye to obtaining admission to

---

[10] Japan, National Diet, *Official Gazette Extra* (English edition), *Minutes of Proceedings in the House of Representatives*, 4th Sess., No. 11, 13 Dec. 1948, pp. 3 and 8.

the United Nations in the future, there was much stress on Japan's acceptance of the ideals of the Organization as stated in the Charter and their close connection with the fervent desire of the Japanese people for peace. A leading article in the newspaper *Asahi* on 14 December 1945 is indicative of this approach:

> Viewed from the standpoint of Japan, it is our belief that the fulfilment of the Potsdam Declaration by Japan, or perhaps we should say, a minimum condition laid down by the Allied Powers, is that all Japanese should strengthen their resolve to do all they can to eradicate war. At the same time, they should carry out the terms of the Potsdam Declaration to the fullest extent while criticizing the recent war and definitely recognizing its crimes. . . . Only such a Japan is competent for membership in and can obtain admission to the United Nations, an organization for world peace.

Secondly, a number of reviews, principally by scholars, analyzed the Charter of the United Nations article by article and compared it with the Covenant of the League of Nations. The merits of the United Nations were highly rated but its inherent weaknesses were also objectively criticized. Kisaburo Yokota (Professor of International Law at Tokyo University) praised the adoption of the general principle of majority rule by the United Nations as marking a brilliant advance in international organization. He wrote:

> The acceptance of the principle of "decision by majority" by the United Nations involves the introduction of a basic principle of democracy into the international community and thereby constitutes progress in the direction of eventual democracy in international life.[11]

Yet, he felt that a compromise and contradiction of this principle was inherent in the Charter provision granting to the Big Five the right of veto in regard to matters before the Security Council. He pointed out that the introduction of the method of decision

[11] Kisaburo Yokota, "The Principle of International Democratic Life," *Sekai*, Jan. 1946.

by seven of the eleven members of the Security Council involved a partial forfeiture of sovereignty on the part of other Security Council members. This repudiation of sovereignty was even more far-reaching for members of the United Nations not represented on the Council, for they were subject to restrictive decisions adopted by the Council without their consent.

> Only the Big Five are exempted from this restriction. . . . As world peace is most likely to be menaced by the bigger nations, to permit the sovereignty of these nations to remain unrestricted, and to allow them a free hand in regard to war prevention, will prove to be a serious obstacle to the maintenance of peace by the United Nations.[12]

On the other hand, there was much praise for the concept of the functions of the United Nations in regard to the peaceful adjustment of international economic and social problems. The magazine *Sekai* argued that peace should be viewed not as a mere static order but as a dynamic state, embodying liberty, justice, and progress in the international community. For this reason, *Sekai* stressed the importance of Article 14 of the Charter under which the General Assembly of the United Nations has the authority to recommend measures for the peaceful adjustment of any situation, regardless of origin, which it deems likely to impair the general welfare or friendly relations among nations. The same magazine drew attention to the significance of the fact that the United Nations Economic and Social Council was separate from the Security Council. In this respect the United Nations was considered a substantial improvement over the League of Nations, which had based its futile efforts to maintain peace on the *status quo*. At the same time it was pointed out that the functions of the United Nations in this field were limited. It could only "recommend" or call for "international co-operation" on economic or social matters.[13]

---

[12] Kisaburo Yokota, "On the World State," *Sekai*, Sept. 1946.

[13] See "The Currents of the World," *Sekai*, May 1946.

The activities of the United Nations began with the hopefully anticipated opening of the first session of the General Assembly in January 1946. The newspaper *Yomiuri* stated on 13 January:

> There is bright hope for the peace of the world which is reflected in the fact that the United States and Britain on the one side and the USSR on the other (between whom conflict seemed inevitable) are shaking hands in the same organization.
>
> The United Nations is a far more powerful organization than the League of Nations was, because the former tries to suppress war throughout the whole world, and may even resort to military force to assure this. The possibility of new aggression is virtually non-existent.

In this same article, however, *Yomiuri* reported on the first rift among the major powers:

> Concerning the election of the President [of the Assembly], unexpected opposition arose between the delegates of the Anglo-American bloc and those of the Soviet satellites on the first day of the General Assembly.

The real international situation soon proved to be far more serious than had been expected. During this period the Iranian and Greek problems became the focus of controversy. The Japanese press, which had at first simply identified hopes for peace with expectations for the United Nations, took cognizance of the serious state of affairs, but nevertheless retained an optimistic outlook toward the United Nations. *Asahi* said on 6 February: "An old struggle for power between Britain and Russia in the East Mediterranean is being revived under the guise of a new situation. . . . Generally speaking, it cannot be expected that the establishment of the United Nations will put an end to power politics." However, it was pointed out that: "The United Nations has provided a golden opportunity to readjust the complicated interests of Great Britain and the Soviet Union through free discussion of Greek and Iranian problems." This statement was overflowing with the expectation that any complication of this nature would somehow be settled because of the opportunity for free discussion provided by the United Nations.

With regard to the tense feeling that arose between Britain and the Soviet Union as a result of the sharp comments which the latter made concerning the stationing of British forces in Greece and Indonesia, *Yomiuri* commented on 10 March:

> It is not strange that complications arise among the nations. The question is whether they can be settled locally after a talk between the countries concerned, or whether both countries cover up their true intentions to the point where the complications become irremediable. Viewed from this angle, the present relationship between the Anglo-American and the Soviet blocs has no such gloomy prospects as is rumored in certain circles, but rather the reverse . . . Should the United States, Great Britain, and the Soviet Union accept and put into operation the suggestion of Secretary of State Byrnes, that when a clash of interests arises, states should make an open confession of their true intentions, present-day international tension would be alleviated in a comparatively simple manner.

*Yomiuri* considered that, after all, international complications can be mitigated and settled provided there is a chance of discussing them in a public forum. The view that "peace has just begun" and accordingly that contemporary conflicts in various parts of the world were, so to speak, "the after-shocks of a great earthquake," was one which *Yomiuri* held in common not only with the Japanese people but also with a large number of people throughout the world who were aspiring for peace.

The international tension which existed at the time of the beginning of the United Nations activities and appeared in the form of a confrontation of Great Britain and the Soviet Union was symbolized by the address delivered in the United States by the former British Prime Minister, Winston Churchill, on 5 March 1946. His impeachment of the Soviet Union was followed by a statement by

Premier Joseph Stalin issued in *Pravda* on 13 March. In spite of the atmosphere of grave opposition produced between the two countries, the Japanese people could still maintain an optimism, based on the existence of the United Nations and the hope that the United States, as the commonly acknowledged leader in the United Nations, could act as an arbitrator between Great Britain and the Soviet Union. This view was held not only in Japan, still under occupation, but was expressed by commentators in other countries as well.

The light of hope was quickly fading away, however, as knotty problems concerning Germany, the Danube, Italy, the Mediterranean, and other parts of Europe, as well as the Middle, Near, and Far East, arose in quick succession. It came to such a pass that the expected arbitrator found itself in head-on collision with the Soviet Union. The opposition between Great Britain and the Soviet Union was becoming overshadowed by the strained relations between the United States and the USSR. When the case of Iran was discussed in the Security Council on 26 March 1946, the Soviet delegate, after a heated debate with the United States representative about the protection of interests of this small nation, left the hall. On 1 April, *Asahi* reported that "the United Nations has been driven into a situation worthy of being called a crisis, the greatest since its founding." On the other hand, when the United Nations began its activities in a new area with the opening of the second session of the Economic and Social Council in May of the same year, *Asahi* on 28 May stressed the enlivening of the "proper charm" of the United Nations by the Economic and Social Council, which was sending forth "fresh air of international co-operation" in contrast to the Security Council which revealed international situations in their negative aspects.

Along with the widespread impression that "peace has just begun," there was the expectation that, even though disputes were arising, they would surely be rectified by open discussion in a universal peace organization such as the United Nations. The grim realities of international politics, however, were moving toward a direct contradiction of this expectation. When disputes arose in rapid succession in various parts of the world, some persons commented that "the after-quakes which frequently come after a great earthquake are quite natural phenomena." This analogy is appropriate for the press of an earthquake country like Japan. But these local disputes were not after-quakes; they were new rumblings of a volcano which unfortunately might disastrously erupt.

Vivid feeling of co-operation prevailed in the days immediately after the war. The United States, Great Britain, and the Soviet Russia had formed a common front in a life and death struggle with the Fascist Axis powers. This gave rise to an easy expectation that these powers could harmoniously engage in the reconstruction of the peace after the war. It may be said that the United Nations was organized on the basis of the expectation that the major powers would work together in the Security Council. But the deep abyss between the Western democracies and communism cannot be bridged by mere good will and negotiation. Their differences are too deeply rooted. Western democracy permits the existence of different ways of thinking in order to further the welfare of the society, approves freedom of speech and thought, makes decisions by majority vote, and decides on future steps on the basis of past experiences. On the contrary, communism is based on the Marxist-Leninist doctrine which does not approve the relativism accepted by capitalism. It tries to break through "the encirclement by capitalist countries" by means of the dictatorship of the proletariat. Good will, negotiation, and agreement during the period immediately after the war played a part in concealing the abyss from the eyes of the people. This could veil the gulf, but had not the power to bridge it. Gusts of wind of real politics blew off veils, one after another, and the people found no bridge on which they could safely cross the abyss. The people, thus disillusioned, referred to this division of the world as "the iron curtain." Quite aside from the question of which party stretched the curtain, the significance lies in the fact that "two worlds" were created despite the efforts of the United Nations to preserve international peace on a universal basis.

The discord of the two worlds still remained an undercurrent during this period and colossal efforts to prevent it from coming to the surface continued. For instance, at the first session of the United Nations General Assembly, the Soviet Foreign Minister, Vyacheslav Molotov, objected to attempts by the small powers to curtail the big power veto and argued that this move was in effect a reactionary offensive against the Soviet Union.[14] Although the United States accused the Soviet Union of abusing the veto power, it did not support the small countries. On this question, *Yomiuri* reprinted an article by Sumner Welles, the former United States Assistant Secretary of State:

> The exercise by the Soviet Union of its veto right has run counter to the spirit of the compromise agreed upon at San Francisco. The protest of the smaller countries has been justified and salutary. Yet the refusal of the General Assembly to take any action beyond registering this protest was altogether wise. The Russian abuse of the veto power is a symptom of a disease. That disease will not be cured at this juncture in world affairs by tampering with the Charter. It will be cured only through a gradual conciliation of the long-range interests of the Soviet Union and of the Western powers.[15]

In these circumstances, the first session of the General Assembly closed and on 3 January 1947 *Yomiuri* quoted Secretary-General Trygve Lie's statement that the horizon had become brighter and international peace seemed to be more assured.[16] The paper attributed the alleviation of the international tension to the *rapprochement* between the United States and the Soviet Union.

---

[14] General Assembly, Official Records (G.A.O.R.): 1st Sess., 2nd Part, 42nd Plenary Mtg., 29 Oct. 1946, p. 838.

[15] Cited in *Yomiuri*, 17 March 1947. Original text in *New York Herald Tribune*, 25 Dec. 1946.

[16] For Lie's statement, see G.A.O.R., 1st Sess., 2nd Part, 67th Plenary Mtg., 15 Dec. 1946, p. 1470.

## VIEWS EXPRESSED IN THE PRESS: 1947-48

The relaxation of international tension lasted for only a brief period. The grim aspects of power politics were soon exposed in one corner of the Balkan peninsula. The attention of the world was drawn to the destiny of Greece, the "solitary island" of Western democracy in the broad Soviet sphere of influence in the Balkans. The United States decision to go to the assistance of Greece marked a turning point in its foreign policy. On 12 March 1947 President Truman announced this policy in the following words:

> One of the primary objectives of the foreign policy of the United States is the creation of conditions in which we and other nations will be able to work out a way of life free from coercion. . . .
>
> We shall not realize our objectives, however, unless we are willing to help free peoples to maintain their free institutions and their national integrity against aggressive movements that seek to impose upon them totalitarian regimes. This is no more than a frank recognition that totalitarian regimes imposed upon free peoples, by direct or indirect aggression, undermine the foundations of international peace and hence the security of the United States.[17]

The President called for a decision by the Congress on assistance to Greece and Turkey in the form of $400 millions credit and the dispatch of military advisers. On the question of United States assistance, *Asahi* on 15 March commented as follows:

> Improvement of international relations in accordance with the principles of justice and international law was the purpose imposed upon . . . the United Nations. Nevertheless, it is a matter of regret that the United Nations and its subsidiary machineries, as President Truman said, are unable to exercise the function of assistance notwithstanding the fact that the emergency in the international situation still continues. It was quite reasonable that the United States bravely took the steps of assistance to Greece and Turkey.

[17] U.S. Dept. of State *Bulletin*, Vol. XVI, No. 403 (23 March 1947), pp. 535-36.

The suddenly aggravated situation in the Balkans was considered to be beyond the power of the United Nations to settle. To acknowledge that there was no course open to the United States but to assist these two countries was tantamount to admitting the hard fact of the existence of two confronting worlds. This "realistic interpretation of the United Nations" was an idea that prevailed in the Japanese press during this period.

The so-called "Truman Doctrine," with its precise definition of the United States platform of anti-communism and its request for assistance for Greece and Turkey, was followed by the Marshall plan, established in order to relieve the critical economic situation in Europe. From the United States point of view, this was a shift from emphasis on the ideological struggle to economic assistance to Europe. At the same time it signalled the strongest counter-offensive so far against communism. Viewed from the Communist side, the Marshall plan meant the pulling down of a "dollar curtain" over Europe, the isolation of Eastern Europe, and the formation of a United States sphere of influence in Europe.[18] Under such circumstances, the "armless war" developed and the confrontation of the two camps was being aggravated continuously. Under these conditions, the *raison d'être* of the United Nations again became a subject of discussion.

*Asahi* reported the situation and stated that gloomy views concerning the United Nations were apparently increasing. Such opinions were held not only in Japan but in many quarters of the world. It could not be denied that there was widespread discontent over the status of the United Nations and, although there were many reasons for this discontent, the main reason was that the Security Council had been unable to solve serious disputes. As a matter of fact, the veto was exercised over twenty times by the Soviet Union and twice by France during the period between the establishment of the United Nations and September 1947 when the second session

[18] See, for example, the speech by the Yugoslav Foreign Minister, Stanoje Simic, G.A.O.R., 2nd Sess., 89th Plenary Mtg., 22 Sept. 1947, p. 236.

of the General Assembly convened. Furthermore, the Soviet Union had frustrated the will of the majority in the Council many times during the same period by threatening to exercise its veto, the so-called "silent veto." On this point, *Asahi* stated on 19 September 1947:

> Aside from the reasons why the veto has been exercised in the Security Council, the cause of the discontent about the Organization must be attributed to the fact that the prompt and peaceful solution of serious problems has been frequently hindered by the veto right of great powers and the fact that there appears to be little likelihood for the pacific settlement of these problems in the near future.

Was there no way then to solve the deadlock which seemed to have been reached in the functioning of the United Nations? The same editorial in *Asahi* continued:

> It is worthy of attention that the United States presented the Greek issue, which had been balked in the Security Council by the exercise of the Soviet veto, to the General Assembly and that the United States is attempting to transfer the center of operations in the United Nations from the Council to the Assembly. If this plan should succeed, the system of establishing peace through the unanimity of the big powers will be replaced by a more democratic system of maintaining peace. The general character of the United Nations will be fundamentally changed since the latter system will place more emphasis on the General Assembly than on the Security Council.

It was admitted that there was some justification for the existing system in that a special responsibility and duty for the maintenance of international peace had been conferred on the big powers by giving them the veto.

*Asahi* anticipated that the excessive use of the veto would be controlled by public opinion through the General Assembly and that this would mark a turning point in the activities of the Organization:

> . . . if the Members of the General Assembly should give an unbiased and proper judgment in the interests of the whole human race and should require the fulfilment of definite decisions, the big powers will be obliged to respect such recommendations. This will have a great influence on the future activities of the Security Council.

In spite of the expectations from various quarters, the schism between the two worlds was deepening and assuming a more complicated and ominous aspect than the simple opposition of the United States and the Soviet Union. On 22 January 1948 Ernest Bevin, Foreign Minister in the British Labour government, called for the consolidation of Western Europe in the light of the breakdown of efforts to co-operate with the Soviet Union. This serious change in the diplomatic policy of Great Britain naturally attracted worldwide attention. The United States, at the same time, clarified its policy toward China and closed the door to a Kuomintang-Communist reconciliation. Then the tragic capitulation of Czechoslovakia occurred. President Truman delivered a special statement to Congress saying that though the United States would devotedly support the Charter of the United Nations, some new action had to be taken with a view to supplementing the activities of the United Nations since pursuit of the purposes of the Charter was hindered "through obstruction and even defiance on the part of one nation."[19] *Asahi* endorsed the President's words that international peace must be earned "not by wishful thinking but by realistic effort."[20] It was felt that people sympathetic to Western democracy would be strongly encouraged by the decisive attitude of the United States. In recommending assistance to Greece and Turkey, President Truman had defined the attitude of the United States and had indicated that the Western democratic system and the way of life in the Soviet Union were incompatible. He implied that the United States would lend its support to any state which,

[19] U.S. Dept. of State *Bulletin*, Vol. XVIII, No. 456 (28 March 1948), p. 419.
[20] *Asahi*, 19 March 1948.

contrary to its desires, was being forced to accept a totalitarian regime. After the coup in Czechoslovakia, the United States reiterated this principle even more forcefully. The spirit of the United Nations and its purposes and principles deserved respect, but it was necessary to admit the fact that the power of the United Nations was limited. Thus, the United States began to avow that, under the existing international situation, the maintenance of peace could be achieved only by "practical power."

Disappointment with the United Nations led to a growing number of plans for changing the Organization. As *Asahi* commented:

> Three years have elapsed since the birth of the United Nations. There are already some people in the world who have pessimistic opinions about the Organization; they feel that unfortunately it will be destined to follow the League of Nations.

In the United States a series of congressional hearings was held in the spring of 1948 to consider proposals for strengthening the United Nations. These proposals represented all shades of opinion. One in particular, submitted in both houses of Congress by members of both the Republican and Democratic parties, was designed to reorganize the United Nations by abolishing the use of the veto on questions of aggression or threats of aggression. The implication was that, if the Soviet Union balked at this plan, the United States should press for the reorganization of the United Nations, even if this meant excluding the Soviet bloc. If this plan had passed the United States Congress and had been submitted to the United Nations, it would have had a serious effect not only on the future of the Organization but also on international peace. It was the intent of the plan to establish an organization without the Soviet Union, if necessary, in which there would be no veto. Fortunately, President Truman and Secretary of State George C. Marshall continued to stress that the United Nations should be supported and that co-operation between the United States and the Soviet Union should be promoted through that Organization.

The sentiment of the Administration and the more moderate elements in Congress prevailed. The House Committee reported favorably on a bill calling for "voluntary action" by the members of the United Nations to liberalize the voting procedure in the Security Council[21] and the Senate passed the Vandenberg Resolution (which the State Department had assisted in drafting) "reaffirming the policy of the United States to achieve international peace . . . through the United Nations," and calling for voluntary action to remove the veto in two areas: pacific settlement of disputes and admission of new members.[22] *Asahi* on 11 May 1948 again commented on the problem as follows:

> So long as the United States maintains its enthusiasm for the United Nations, it is clear that the Organization will continue to exist and in the long run it will assume a role which will answer the world's expectations for peace. The Soviet Union also seems to regard the United Nations as the best peace organization under contemporary conditions in the world.

This same editorial stated that, although the present United Nations was enmeshed in controversy, it had to be supported and *Asahi* expressed its faith in the healthy growth of the United Nations in the future.

In June 1948 the "Berlin blockade" was instituted and under the shadow of the aggravated relations between East and West, the third session of the General Assembly opened in Paris on 21 September. On this occasion, *Asahi* admonished its readers not to be disappointed too hastily in the United Nations, and asserted that, notwithstanding its seeming powerlessness, the important functions the Organization performed in the present international society should

---

[21] U.S. House of Representatives, 80th Cong., 2nd Sess , *Report of the Ctte. on Foreign Affairs on H.R. 6802: United Nations Participation Act* (Washington: Govt. Printing Office, 1948), p. 42. No further action was taken by the House on this bill.

[22] U.S. Senate, 80th Cong., 2nd Sess., Senate Resolution 239, 11 June 1948. The text of this resolution also appears in U.S. Dept. of State *Bulletin*, Vol. XIX, No. 472 (18 July 1948), p. 79. See also below, pp. 111-12.

be calmly evaluated. According to this newspaper, various efforts were being made in order to find a way out of the impasse, for instance, the movement of the United World Federalists. But, if hasty action to realize such aims were taken it would inevitably, in the practical world of politics, cause the withdrawal of the Soviet Union from the United Nations and consequently the "one world" would be split in two.

On this point, *Asahi* commented as follows: "Although the United Nations is powerless in settling the present conflicts between the United States and the Soviet Union and between East and West Germany, the world situation would be more unstable if the United Nations did not exist." Therefore, the function of maintaining world peace should be "nourished not outside but inside of the womb."

> As the problem shall pass the strait gate of the veto, the labor pain will be long and intolerable. But if a fetus is extracted too hastily, the mother's body will be harmed. Moreover, the people are gradually understanding that the problem of the world peace organization requires the utmost patience.

*Yomiuri* shared the view that actions which might bring a split in the United Nations should be avoided even though the Organization could not answer the world's expectations. "There are some reasons for pessimism concerning the United Nations, it is true, but under the conditions of the present-day world, the United Nations is the only ligament that ties the two split worlds together."

*Sekai*, in its September 1948 issue, published an article entitled "The Crisis of the United Nations." While pointing out that the United Nations had made important contributions in the economic and social fields, the article stressed its lack of accomplishments in the political field.

> Now, the United Nations is compelled to decide whether the Organization shall deal only with rather simple and secondary matters or shall deal with serious problems notwithstanding the danger of failure. It seems that the Organization has

> bravely chosen the latter course. We have to pay respect to its resolute attitude; however, we cannot but be disappointed when the results of its effort are examined.
>
> In the field of international political relations, in which the Organization should have performed its main function, it has failed to bring about satisfactory effects. Even though the Organization has not succeeded in reaching practical solutions of these matters, there are some people who point out the significance of the fact that disputed matters have been dealt with by international machinery such as the United Nations and discussed under the superintendence of the public opinion of the world. There is some merit in this view, but the people of the world expect the Organization to be something more than a forum for exchange of international opinions and to be an instrument by which international problems are solved peacefully and rationally in accordance with the common wish for peace. In other words, they expect the Organization to develop into a higher authority, able to control the arbitrary activities of sovereign states in the interests of world peace.

The third session of the General Assembly, held in the threatening atmosphere resulting from the Berlin problem, was at first surrounded by an aura of pessimism, but later assumed a more hopeful air. Fortunately, Secretary-General Trygve Lie's prediction that the United Nations might face the most serious crisis it ever had, did not come true. One reason for this was that the Western powers were very cautious in dealing with the Berlin problem. They did not submit the problem to the General Assembly and thus did not drive the Soviet Union into a corner. But there was another reason; the small countries carried on a vigorous activity in the General Assembly. Concerning this, *Mainichi* commented as follows:

> The spiritless and pessimistic atmosphere surrounding the opening of the General Assembly faded as the conference proceeded, mainly because of the vigorous activities of the small countries. The small powers overwhelm the big powers in numbers. Of the fifty-eight members of the United Nations, fifty-three are the so-called "small powers." They have greater

> reason than do great powers to wish that the United Nations adequately carry out its function of maintaining peace and security. The big countries have the power to defend themselves, but the small states do not. It is quite reasonable that the small powers should bend their efforts to see that the United Nations does not fall into an irretrievable crisis. The small powers are not desperate about the powerlessness of the United Nations which has been due mainly to the veto of the big countries, and their active efforts are to be commended in the interests of the United Nations itself as well as in the interests of international peace.[23]

As *Asahi* also had pointed out, "the effort of the small states to maintain the peace not outside but inside, and through, the United Nations should be fully appreciated."[24]

Along with these opinions concerning the role of the small powers, there were many others which cautioned against desperation about the United Nations and endeavored to seek a modest but indisputable *raison d'être* for the Organization. These opinions and attitudes showed that the Japanese intellectuals at this time had a proper recognition and evaluation of the United Nations.

[23] *Mainichi*, editorial of 12 Dec. 1948 entitled "The General Assembly and the Activities of the Small States."

[24] *Asahi*, 27 Sept. 1948.

*chapter three*

# The Second Period: Rise of Neutralism

(January 1949—May 1950)

Newspapers in Japan reported on 3 March 1949 that General MacArthur, then the Supreme Commander for the Allied Powers, in an interview with a correspondent of the London *Daily Mail*, had stated that the United States wished that Japan would remain neutral in the event war broke out and become the Switzerland of the Pacific.[1] This statement was a strong incentive to the Japanese nation to adopt a resolute stand in favor of a policy of permanent neutrality. The adoption of such a position would imply the intention of keeping the drift of contemporary international politics in check, and of preventing Japan from becoming either antagonistic toward, or unduly receptive to, regional collective security arrangements such as a Pacific alliance. The discussion concerning the possibility and desirability of permanent neutrality for Japan was carried out in the Japanese press and in the Diet.

[1] See *The New York Times*, 2 March 1949.

## DISCUSSION IN THE DIET

Support for a position of permanent neutrality was prevalent chiefly in the political parties not represented in the Yoshida government, especially those of progressive inclination. The issue of permanent neutrality and the possibility of a Pacific pact was the subject of remarks in the House of Councillors in April 1949. Kei Hoashi, who later became a member of the Socialist party, said:

> With what we suffered from the atomic bomb Japan should be proud of having abandoned her armaments and, keeping aloof from all international disputes, should enjoy a permanent neutrality no less than Sweden or Switzerland.[2]

He demanded that the government make its position clear on this point. Takaharu Ito, presuming that the terms of the proposed Pacific pact were similar to those of the North Atlantic pact, argued that participation in such an alliance would mean that Japan might become involved in a war in case of an attack on any of its allies. This would be in violation of the Constitution and would be inconsistent with Japan's desire to become the Switzerland of the Pacific.[3]

The government's answers to these questions were literally prudent and Yoshida's remarks were not always compatible with the Supreme Commander's words. Using Belgium as an example of a country which became involved in a war despite a recognized position of permanent neutrality, Yoshida replied to Hoashi, "I have some doubt as to whether it is right and proper for our country to declare perpetual neutrality. . . . It is a matter deserving careful consideration."[4] He went on to point out that the United Nations had been given the authority to decide upon the imposition of

---

[2] Japan, National Diet, *Official Gazette Extra* (English edition), *Minutes of Proceedings in the House of Councillors*, 5th Sess., No. 11, 7 April 1949, p. 20. Hereinafter referred to as *Proceedings in the House of Councillors.*

[3] *Ibid.*, pp. 26-27.

[4] *Ibid.*, p. 22.

military restraints upon an aggressor and to bind the members of the Organization by that decision. Such a position was at least theoretically incompatible with a concept of permanent neutrality which would permit neutrals of any description to remain apart from international disputes. Therefore, insofar as Japan may depend upon the collective security system of the United Nations and desire eagerly to join the Organization, it is inconsistent for Japan to be the Switzerland of the Pacific.

The Premier avoided an answer to Hoashi's demand for cautiousness in connection with a Pacific pact. On the other hand, in replying to Ito, he alleged that if a treaty such as NATO, which was established to oppose the aggression of the Communist powers, should come into effect in the Pacific, disarmed Japan would be unable to join it. It would be incompatible with the idea of permanent neutrality to admit that a regional agreement such as NATO might be necessary as part of the collective security system of the United Nations. If the treaty aimed only at the establishment of international peace, however, Japan should become a party to it in order to contribute to peace in the Far East.[5] This is worthy of note as a manifestation of Yoshida's willingness to approve Japan's participation in a regional arrangement directed toward maintaining peace.

It was not until the 6th Session of the Diet in the autumn of 1949 that much was said in favor of permanent neutrality. Again, this view was particularly emphasized by the Socialist and Workers and Farmers parties. As people were becoming more conscious that the idea of permanent neutrality might be incompatible with that of collective security as envisioned by the United Nations, they came eventually to the conclusion that Japan's participation in the United Nations might not be so easily achieved as had been hoped in the preceding period. Hisao Kuroda of the Workers and Farmers party and Kei Hoashi both insisted that instead of advocating collective security, which was likely to involve Japan in the "cold

---

[5] *Ibid.*, p. 28.

war" and might make the country a battlefield in case war broke out, Japan should advance in the direction of permanent neutrality and adhere to the spirit of renunciation of war. Naoki Hoshino of the Workers and Farmers party, in particular, maintained that Japan should adopt a policy of permanent neutrality rather than seek to participate in the United Nations if it were considered that the Charter hampers the admission of a permanently neutral state. He emphasized that his assertion implied a demand for revision of the Charter of the United Nations. He said:

> If we put forward the collective security system in our eagerness to join the United Nations, this will only serve to disturb the nation's aspiration for eternal peace.[6]

He pressed the government to state whether it was ready to call for a plebiscite on the alternatives of permanent neutrality and active participation in a collective security system.

Yoshida remained silent throughout these interpellations, merely pleading that permanent neutrality could not become a subject of discussion at that time, since the problem was still an abstract one. Similarly, the government evaded answering a request made during this session of the Diet that the armed forces of a specific state be stationed in Japan for the sake of its security. Michio Matsui of the Ryokufukai[7] stated in the House of Councillors that the ideal method for safeguarding Japan's security would be through the United Nations but he doubted that the United Nations was "adequately prepared" to give the necessary assurances. He remarked: "We have no alternative but to rely on the well-disposed Powers for our national security . . . It may be unavoidable to have American forces stationed in Japan."[8] To this Yoshida replied: "I would refrain from giving comments . . . on this occasion."[9]

---

[6] *Ibid.*, 6th Sess., No. 12, 16 Nov. 1949, p. 2.

[7] The Ryokufukai (Green Breeze Society) is an organization of Conservative members of the House of Councillors.

[8] *Proceedings in the House of Councillors*, No. 12, 16 Nov. 1949, p. 4.

[9] *Ibid.*, p. 6.

This remark should be taken as a manifestation of the weak and delicate position of the Prime Minister of a state which, while under Allied occupation, was drawn into the vortex of subtle international relationships.

Although the government gave no responsive answers concerning national policy on these vital problems of international relations, fairly definite explanations were given on theoretical problems of international law. The deliberations in the 6th Session of the Diet on the hypothetical problem of admission to the United Nations focussed upon the following two questions:

1. Is it possible for a neutral state to join the United Nations?
2. Would not the spirit of the Constitution with its provisions for the renunciation of arms be inconsistent with the duty of offering armed forces which membership in the Organization would impose upon Japan?

In answer to a question on these points raised by one of the members of the Foreign Affairs Committee of the Diet, government officials (mainly Kumao Nishimura, Chief of the Treaty Bureau of the Foreign Office) gave explanations sufficiently theoretical to leave out actual political considerations. The government's position was roughly as follows:

To study the problem of the relations between the United Nations and neutral states, it is essential to distinguish between "permanent neutrality" and "neutrality as a diplomatic policy." By "permanent neutrality" is meant a state which enters into an agreement with adjacent nations that it will remain permanently neutral in any war imaginable in the future on condition that, in return, the neutrality of the said state is respected and left inviolable by those nations. Such a stand of permanent neutrality is understood to be incompatible with the United Nations manner of settling international disputes. On the other hand, "neutrality as a diplomatic policy" is a government policy of attempting to remain apart from controversies among other nations. This on no account conflicts directly with the position of that particular nation as a member of the United Nations.

Whether the spirit of the Japanese Constitution (which provides for renunciation of arms) can be consistent with the duty of providing military forces as required by the United Nations Charter was, in the government's opinion, a question to be settled on the basis of a specific decision by the Security Council. Even if the need for military action should arise, the measures called for by that Council would not be the same for all members of the United Nations, but would vary according to circumstances. Consequently, it is not likely that any such decision would demand belligerent actions by a totally unarmed nation. The only demand imaginable would be for economic co-operation, approval of passage of troops through the land, and adoption of other similar policies insofar as they are compatible with the position of an unarmed nation. This is clear from the fact that Iceland, which has no army, navy, or air force, has been admitted to the United Nations.

According to the government's interpretation, consistent adherence to the stand of permanent neutrality is incompatible with membership in the United Nations. These alternatives are mutually exclusive. Nevertheless, any state may join the United Nations without departing from a neutral policy and an unarmed state is not hindered from joining the United Nations. Permanent neutrality and a neutral policy are two different things. The government warned against considering that Japan's participation in the United Nations was easily possible and pointed out that Japan's actual position and the United Nations admission procedure rendered such participation extremely difficult.

Some minority members argued that Japan could, without violating its unarmed pacifism, participate in the United Nations if an exception could be made for Japan in the United Nations rules for applying "sanctions." However, they had some misgivings about the government's explanation that Japan's unarmed pacifism and the duty to provide armed forces, which would be a natural concomitant of admission to the United Nations, are by no means conflicting concepts. Mrs. Togano of the Socialist party, for instance, demanded that the basic principle of unarmed neutrality, as set forth in the new Constitution, be strictly observed. She felt that any attempt to lower esteem for the new Constitution, even in order to join the United Nations, involved retrogression, and not progress, in international politics. The total lack of any intention on the part of the government at that time to effect rearmament is clear from Prime Minister Yoshida's frequent statements. At the time of these political developments, the government might well be said to have had high hopes that the door of the United Nations would be opened to an unarmed Japan. Yet, despite the government's evasive attitude toward the alternatives of permanent neutrality and collective security, the tendency to favor the latter seemed to be increasing.

In 1950, the 7th Session of the Diet opened against the background of an international situation which was taking a turn for the worse and which culminated in the outbreak of the Korean War. One of the outstanding features of the session was that the government, which had maintained that renunciation of war involved virtual renunciation of the right of self-defense, suddenly began to show an affirmative attitude toward such a right. Yoshida, in his speech on the government's policy in the plenary session of the House of Representatives on 23 January said, "Renunciation of war does not mean abandonment of the right of self defense."[10] His statement created an immediate sensation in various circles; numerous interpellations were focussed on this point to ascertain what the Prime Minister meant by the right of self-defense. The answers by government spokesmen revealed that what they had in mind was by no means rearmament, but the affirmation by Japan of its right to self-defense notwithstanding its drastic policy of renunciation of war. The principle enunciated was that "the security

[10] Japan, National Diet, *Official Gazette Extra* (English edition), *Minutes of Proceedings in the House of Representatives*, 7th Sess., No. 11, 23 Jan. 1950, p. 2.

of Japan depends on gaining international confidence for Japan's peaceful, democratic intentions."[11]

Some of the members of the non-government parties took the government to task for this ambiguous attitude toward security. They felt it implied that Japan would remain unarmed and national defense left to the forces of other countries. They asserted that for Japan to provide bases for foreign countries would be contrary to the spirit of the Constitution. The government's new attitude may be seen as a step taken in anticipation of a defensive system such as later materialized in the Security Treaty between Japan and the United States. The government cleverly parried this hail of queries; Yoshida stated, "As to the problem of military base[s], I shall reserve my answer, as we have received no intimation of the matter."[12]

The United Nations was scarcely brought into this discussion on the right of self-defense. One exception was a speech by Yoshio Namiki of the Democratic party who asked in a meeting of the Foreign Affairs Committee of the House of Representatives on 21 December 1949 if it were not possible for the United Nations to settle international disputes involving non-members of the Organization. In reply, a government member of the Committee, referring to Article 2(6) and Article 35 of the Charter of the United Nations, stated, "We understand that the door to the United Nations is kept open even for non-members of the Organization."[13]

The fact that the government in this period clearly adopted an affirmative view of the right of self-defense reflected actual developments in the international situation. On 14 February 1950 the Soviet Union and Communist China concluded a treaty which set forth the determination of the two countries to co-operate and act jointly to prevent " . . . a repetition of aggression on the part of

---

[11] *Proceedings in the House of Councillors*, 7th Sess., No. 14, 30 Jan. 1950, p. 4.

[12] *Ibid.*, No. 15, 31 Jan. 1950, p. 19.

[13] Japan, National Diet, Foreign Affairs Ctte. of the House of Representatives, 6th Sess., 21 Dec. 1949 (author's translation).

Japan or any other state which should unite in any form with Japan in acts of aggression."[14] The terminology of this clause was a surprise to the Japanese people. They believed themselves to be utterly powerless, yet clearly Japan and the powers backing Japan were viewed as the imaginary enemies. Indeed this fact was enough to convince the Japanese government and people that "good will" could not be expected from the Soviet Union or Communist China. The alliance implied the possibility of an attack on Japan on the pretext of self-defense against Japan's attempted "aggressions." It was necessary for Japan to provide in some way or other against this contingency and it was for this reason that the question of approval of the right of self-defense took precedence over all others. These considerations perhaps explain the government's abrupt support in the Diet of the right of self-defense, despite the provisions in the Constitution for disarmament.

## PUBLIC OPINION AND PERMANENT NEUTRALITY

At the beginning of 1949, the tension of the "cold war" was still increasing but, at the same time, a tremendous effort was being made to avoid war. Placed between the tense opposition of the two powers and without any position as an independent state in international society, Japan was feeling great anxiety about its future. In such a situation, General Douglas MacArthur's statement that the United States hoped that Japan would become the Switzerland of the Pacific made an extraordinary impression on the Japanese people. There would be nothing more desirable for the Japanese people than to stand apart from all the conflicts and disputed matters by preserving permanent neutrality. In an editorial entitled, "The Way to Permanent Neutrality," *Asahi* commented as follows:

---

[14] For text, see Raymond Dennett and Robert K. Turner (eds.) *Documents on American Foreign Relations* (Princeton: Published for World Peace Foundation by Princeton University Press, 1951), Vol. XII, 1950, pp. 518-519.

> Japan, under the supervision of the Occupation forces, is not recognized in its legitimate position as an independent state and is not permitted to join the United Nations. This is the result of the unfortunate split between the two great powers which developed shortly after the war. . . . Japan, placed between the two big powers, must be determined to preserve a neutral position however the international situation may develop. . . . There is no other way than permanent neutrality for the Japanese who have declared their renunciation of war. It is high time now for Japan to stabilize and regularize domestic conditions in order to maintain permanent neutrality.

*Yomiuri* upheld the same stand, stating: "A pacific state which has abandoned armed force has no other choice than to preserve its neutrality."[15]

Many Japanese had a vague hope that Japan could adopt a policy of permanent neutrality and at the same time gain admission to the United Nations. When Premier Yoshida, in a radio broadcast on 2 September 1949, stated that the only way to preserve the territory and independence of Japan was to show a determination to maintain international peace by entering the United Nations, *Mainichi* commented as follows:[16]

> Mr. Yoshida, the Prime Minister, declared that the Japanese should fulfil their responsibility for preserving world peace by entering the United Nations. This statement may be overlooked as a very common one but is really an important declaration as it involves complicated questions.

Pointing out that many Japanese found no inconsistency between permanent neutrality and entrance into the United Nations, the editorial observed:

> It is likely that the Japanese vaguely think that these two positions will doubly protect them. There exists, however, a contradiction between the two. That is why the Prime Minister's

[15] *Asahi*, 3 March 1949, and *Yomiuri*, 9 April 1949.

[16] "Admission to the United Nations and Permanent Neutrality," *Mainichi*, 4 Sept. 1949.

> statement has such grave significance. Permanent neutrality is a negative position taken to evade involvement in international disputes. On the other hand, when admitted to the United Nations, a state must act in accordance with the decisions of the Organization concerning international disputes.

Concluding that the position of the United Nations or that of its members cannot be neutral, *Mainichi* raised the question whether Japan's policy was to be directed toward entrance into the United Nations rather than toward permanent neutrality.

> Permanent neutrality may be of doubtful effectiveness against aggression and also may be a kind of international individualism. Yet, has Japan the capacity to discharge its duties for maintaining world peace if it is admitted to the United Nations? Of course, the function of the United Nations does not merely lie in the maintenance of security by force. It may be argued that Japan should enter the United Nations with a view to participating in international co-operation. But, as a consequence of this, is it proper to abandon permanent neutrality? The question is more serious if it means that Japan should enter the security system of the United Nations and at the same time sacrifice its stand of permanent neutrality in order to oppose the presupposed military attack of some imaginary enemy.

In pointing out that permanent neutrality and entrance into the United Nations were not as compatible as people seemed to think, this *Mainichi* editorial was critical of the attitude of the government. It was in the nature of a warning against taking as a matter of course the desire to join the United Nations since this step would inevitably lead Japan toward entanglements. This represented the feeling of those Japanese intellectuals who hesitated to join either side in the conflict of the two opposing worlds.

While the Constitution of Japan, which stipulates the renunciation of all armed force and the nullification of the right of belligerency, may be construed in such a way as to include the principle of permanent neutrality, what would be the outcome if Japan tried to stick to a position of permanent neutrality? If the disarmed pacifism of the Constitution and the principle of permanent neutrality were firmly maintained, what would be the result if Japan were attacked? The magazine *Chuo-Koron* observed: "In the present international situation where order and the machinery of world peace is not yet established, a small defeated nation wishing to stick with resolve to a policy of permanent neutrality must have a religious determination not to resort to armed force even though the land be turned to ashes and the whole nation be wounded or die."[17] These words may be interpreted in two ways: either that, in spite of the absence of world peace, Japan must observe permanent neutrality; or that the desirability and possibility of permanent neutrality is questionable. This article, together with the editorial of *Mainichi*, played a part in calling the attention of the people, who vaguely linked permanent neutrality with admission to the United Nations, to the fact that the situation was not an easy one.

While the press questioned whether it was really possible or proper for Japan, having declared for disarmed pacifism, to seek security by admission to the United Nations, the Diet engaged in debates which presupposed the admission of Japan to the United Nations and the public took it all as a matter of course. *Asahi* referred to this discussion in an editorial on 2 November entitled "Extremely Easy-Going Questions and Answers."

It was pointed out that the questions in the Foreign Affairs Committee of the House of Representatives and the answers of the government to them did not go beyond a primitive interpretation of the United Nations Charter. The fact could not be overlooked that the debates tacitly admitted that entrance into the United Nations was the basis of Japan's policy and in effect implied that neutrality is difficult to observe but admission to the United Nations is easy. *Asahi* questioned whether it was really easy to enter the United Nations. First, the exercise of the veto is an obstacle to the

[17] "Permanent Neutrality and Defense of the Country," *Chuo-Koron*, June 1949.

accomplishment of this step and the issue becomes even more difficult if the country in question is involved in any conflict between East and West. Stating that if Japan concluded a separate peace treaty with the West, admission to the United Nations could not be expected, the editorial then commented:

> It is dangerous to discuss the question [of Japan's future] under the premise of admission to the United Nations. First of all, it is necessary to examine the fundamental problem whether collective security, by way of admission to the United Nations, will guarantee real peace to Japan or whether permanent neutrality will adequately serve this purpose. Which method will be better fitted to carry out the spirit of the new Constitution of Japan? Despite the fact that it is impossible to achieve 100 per cent safety anywhere under the menacing situations of the world, which method would protect the Japanese people and thus contribute to international peace? This must be the gauge used in choosing between the two alternatives.

This editorial gave a warning to the government and the Foreign Affairs Committee which were indulging in superficial discussions. At the same time, *Asahi* stated that Japan, in the unique status of having no armed forces, "can demand a special right in appealing to the world for peace and self-defense." Thus, in effect, the editorial expressed an attitude generally inclined toward disarmed neutralism.

*Asahi* asked scholars of international law to give their opinions on the question of the compatibility of permanent neutrality and participation in a collective security system. The paper printed two essays, one by Professor Kisaburo Yokota (Tokyo University), who supported collective security, and another by Professor Ryoichi Taoka (Kyoto University), who took the side of permanent neutrality.[18]

Professor Yokota's views were as follows: There are two methods to insure the security of Japan, one of which must be the keypoint of a peace treaty. The one is security underwritten by a specific

[18] See *Asahi*, 10 and 11 Nov. 1949.

country and the other is security through international peace machinery. The method of permanent neutrality will, in the long run, give way to one or the other of these two alternatives, as there is probably no guarantee that Japan will not be attacked despite its declared neutrality. If the first method is adopted, Japan and the specified country would be in effect an indivisible entity. In the case of the second method, Japan would maintain the status of an independent state under normal conditions but would come under the protection of the United Nations in case of attack. However, effective action by the United Nations would be unlikely owing to the veto and, in fact, Japan would have to be protected by those countries that recognize the necessity for the security and independence of Japan. If such protection is considered neither certain nor dependable, there is another course open to Japan: the establishment of regional peace machinery to which Japan might adhere. These are the choices which will decide the destiny of Japan.

This theory of Professor Yokota is based on a realistic analysis of the international position of Japan. Later, in concluding the Security Treaty with the United States, Japan selected the first method as defined by Professor Yokota—security by alliance with a specified country.

Professor Taoka, on the other hand, advocated the idea of permanent neutrality. He stressed that the United Nations cannot perform its security functions because of the veto. Consequently, members of the United Nations have no alternative but to seek security by establishing organizations outside of the United Nations. Such organizations may try to avoid being classified as alliances, but that is what, in effect, they are. Security arrangements of this nature cause uneasiness and fear on the part of the country against which the alliance seems directed and this leads to organized counter-alliances. Thus, the world splits into two groups of countries. Under such circumstances, it is natural for a country in the middle that has no armed forces to adhere to a position of permanent neutrality. The unreliability of security through the United Nations supports the argument in favor of permanent neutrality. While it also invites the idea of insuring security by means of alliances with other countries, Article 9 of the Constitution of Japan is an obstacle to this course of action. Moreover, an alliance between an economically weak and disarmed country, such as Japan, and a great power would not be an equal alliance but rather a protectorate. Therefore, for a small country desiring to have its security assured by other countries, it is more advantageous to be protected by many countries, including members of both the conflicting groups. This consideration naturally leads to support for the idea of permanent neutrality.

Generally speaking, Professor Taoka's views probably received greater sympathy from Japanese intellectuals than did Professor Yokota's.

Among the general public, opinion seems to have been equally divided between support for permanent neutrality and advocacy of Japan's joining the United Nations. A public opinion poll carried out by *Asahi* at the end of 1949 produced the following results: 39% of those interviewed favored a policy of permanent neutrality; 36% advocated Japan's joining the United Nations; 7% felt Japan should rely on a regional collective security arrangement; 8% favored an agreement with a particular country such as the United States; and 10% expressed no opinion. Those favoring permanent neutrality felt that Japan could thereby avoid becoming involved in a war; opposition to such a policy was based on the belief that it would not be effective. Various reasons were given for joining the United Nations: that Japan could thereby contribute to world peace; that this was a step toward world government; that the world situation required that Japan join the Organization. Those who opposed membership in the United Nations argued that this would involve Japan in international disputes and perhaps in a war and they also emphasized the incompatibility of membership in the United Nations and the renunciation of war in the Constitution.

In February 1950, before any decision on the international position of Japan had been reached, the Soviet Union and Communist China concluded their treaty of alliance, which openly treated Japan as a possible enemy.[19] Under these circumstances it became more and more unrealistic for Japan to continue to aspire to a position of permanent neutrality.

## PRESS VIEWS ON THE UNITED NATIONS

In the light of the delicate question of the compatibility of United Nations membership and permanent neutrality, the principal newspapers of Japan showed a hesitant attitude in concluding that Japan should join the United Nations. After October 1949, however, the trend in newspaper editorials turned markedly toward support for this move. On 25 October, in an editorial in commemoration of the fourth anniversary of the coming into effect of the United Nations Charter, *Mainichi* commented that "the fact that the United Nations exists and is active holds hopes for the world." It went on to say that while there are various problems to be considered by Japan in relation to its desire for peace and its preference for perpetual neutrality, as a matter of principle Japan should think about joining the United Nations and about doing its share for the preservation of world peace.

The same editorial drew attention to the fact that the General Assembly at its previous session had adopted the Universal Declaration of Human Rights:

> The substance of human rights and liberty referred to [in the Universal Declaration] is that of democracy as opposed to totalitarianism. The Soviet Union abstained from voting at the time the General Assembly adopted the declaration. It was made clear that the United Nations is not aloof from the conflicting ideologies in reality but that the ideology of United Nations is that of democracy. Therefore, the efforts of the United Nations are directed toward settling international

[19] See above, pp. 43-44.

> problems not by empty compromises, but rather on the basis of democratic principles. This makes the tasks of the Organization all the more difficult but at the same time makes their efforts nobler.

This editorial observation is noteworthy, for *Mainichi* had previously been emphasizing the desirability of neutralism for Japan. In this appreciable departure from its former position, *Mainichi* was moving toward support for the United Nations as an international peace organization.

During the fourth session of the United Nations General Assembly, which opened on 20 September 1949, the United Nations took unmistakable steps toward realism and away from idealism. Instead of discussing general proposals, such as bringing an end to the "cold war," efforts were directed toward settlement of various specific issues. Attention was focused on technical programs which the United Nations could carry out, rather than on high-level discussion of United Nations ideals. From one viewpoint, this reflected the fact that the opposition between East and West had come to an irretrievable impasse. But from another viewpoint it also meant that in the light of stark reality the United Nations started its forward advance toward peace by dealing with problems which it was capable of tackling, albeit problems which were neither spectacular nor high-sounding. This change in approach was graphically described by the Philippine delegate, Carlos Romulo, who explained that while the United Nations was not empowered to move or level a mountain, it could build a small pass toward harmony beyond the mountain. Quoting this statement, *Asahi* observed on 26 September 1949:

> The United Nations, by opening a narrow passage even if it can not move a mountain, shows its new resolve to tackle international politics realistically, by discarding its initial dreams. . . . It must be now increasingly clear to the United Nations that the ideal of moving a mountain cannot by itself remove the opposition.

The newspaper *Yomiuri*, in a number of editorials, expressed concern over the crisis the United Nations was facing. An editorial dated 12 December 1949, for instance, observed that "the atmosphere in the United Nations today bears an astonishing resemblance to that of the League of Nations on the eve of its crisis." It continued:

> The atmosphere of international politics which appeared to have taken a turn for the better around the summer of this year is getting increasingly worse because of, or rather in spite of, the fact that the supreme organ of the United Nations is in session. These meetings seem to show in close-up the inherent danger to the United Nations itself.

*Yomiuri* also commented on the attempt to shift the center of gravity from the Security Council, where the great power veto was the stumbling block, to the General Assembly, which is based on the principle of formalistic equality in voting—that is, each member having one vote. But, *Yomiuri* pointed out, the Assembly is far more impotent than the Council in dealing with serious issues, since the Assembly has no power to call for direct action by the members of the United Nations. Furthermore, the General Assembly "is apt to become an arena of propaganda," where "every evil of open diplomacy is presented in a magnified form." With the decision to shift the center of United Nations activities to the General Assembly, the people "are preoccupied with preserving the form of the Organization and while they are under the impression that the United Nations is still sound, its structure is faced with the peril of losing its power to solve practical problems and it may become petrified."

It is interesting to note that despite these pessimistic comments on the actual conditions of the United Nations, *Yomiuri*, in an editorial on 21 December, pointed out that a resolution for aiding underdeveloped regions was unanimously approved at the fourth session of the General Assembly and the hope was expressed that "an atmosphere of cheerful co-operation may be generated from an economic aspect."

*chapter four*

# The Third Period: The Korean War

(June 1950—February 1951)

With the outbreak of the Korean War, the United Nations was put to its severest test. The measures it took for the sake of collective security resulted in a fierce "hot war" which, although local in scale, presented every danger of developing into a conflict of world proportions should the wrong course be taken. Japan, a country separated from the Korean peninsula by only a narrow strait, was keenly aware that the resolute steps taken by the United Nations were at the same time contributing to the defense of Japan.

A survey regarding the attitude of Japanese political parties concerning United Nations problems revealed that the Liberal party, which was still in power with an overwhelming majority in the House of Representatives, believed that the armed action taken by the United Nations was quite justified. The Liberals demanded maximum co-operation with the United Nations forces at the Korean front. They looked to the Organization for Japan's security, and vehemently supported Japan's admission to the United Nations. The Democratic party (later the Progressive party) took a similar stand in support of co-operation with the United Nations. The Democrats, however, had growing doubts that the United Nations system of collective security would be adequate. This may be considered a prelude to the policy of rearmament on which they later took the initiative. Though supporting Japan's neutrality, the Socialist party showed an approbatory and co-operative attitude toward the actions of the United Nations. The Socialists maintained that Japan should join a collective security system on a worldwide scale but should not take a positive part in possible armed actions of the United Nations. The Communist party naturally denounced the military measures of the United Nations in Korea as aggressive action of United States imperialism. Within the government and among a great many members of the Diet, there was a tendency toward a shift from the highly idealistic peace worship of the earlier period to support for the Western bloc in the United Nations, with the United States as its main pillar.

## DISCUSSION IN THE DIET

When the 8th (Emergency) Session of the Diet opened on 13 July 1950, the first issue brought forward was the measures taken by the United Nations against the North Korean Communist forces. Yoshida gave this action his total approval in his speech in the Diet on 14 July:

> It is heartening . . . that America and so many other members of the United Nations have gone to the rescue of the invaded country regardless of the heavy sacrifice involved. In case a war breaks out on an extensive scale how could Japan's security be preserved [since we are disarmed]? . . . This has been the point hotly discussed. However, the measure taken by the United Nations has done much in stabilizing our people's minds. . . . Japan, though not in a position to play a positive role, will cooperate within the limits of her ability.

> In the face of the current situation . . . the proposals put forward such as the so-called "over-all peace", "neutrality", or "non-involvement" . . . ignore reality . . .[1]

Disputes in the Diet developed as to what was meant by Yoshida's phrase, co-operation with the United Nations. According to his own interpretation, it meant not only that Japan should "offer support" to United Nations actions but also "extend spiritual co-operation" even though Japan was not qualified for participation in the positive actions of the United Nations.[2] This rather vague expression brought forth a volley of critical questions from the left and the right wings. The attack by the extreme left was exemplified by Yasoji Kazahaya of the Communist party, who demanded an immediate abandonment of what he called the government's "war cooperation policy."[3] On behalf of the right wing, on the contrary, Yoichi Kawaguchi of the Farmers Co-operative party made a demand which implied rearmament. He stated that the seriousness of the Far Eastern situation called for more than "spiritual cooperation" on Japan's part. He asked, "Is it improper for us to think of cultivating strength sufficient to defend ourselves?"[4] The government's reply was that there was no other alternative than to use the expression "cooperating spiritually with the United Nations," since Japan was not yet in a position to call up volunteer forces.

Regarding the increasing number of military bases for the United Nations forces in Japan due to the Korean War, the government stated:

> It is . . . a treaty obligation that . . . our country . . . should cooperate with the Occupation Forces whenever the latter requests some equipment for the occupation purposes. It is

[1] Japan, National Diet, *Official Gazette Extra* (English edition), *Minutes of Proceedings in the House of Representatives*, 8th Sess., No. 3, 14 July 1950, p. 2. Hereinafter referred to as *Proceedings in the House of Representatives.*

[2] *Ibid.*, No. 4, 15 July 1950, p. 8.

[3] *Ibid.*, No. 5, 17 July 1950, p. 15.

[4] *Ibid.*, pp. 16-17.

> up to the occupying countries, therefore, how those facilities which were established through our cooperation are used.[5]

In other words, provision of the bases was accounted for not as a manifestation of co-operation with the United Nations but as a duty of an occupied state. Under these circumstances, the Police Reserves were established in Japan in August. This was the first step toward virtual rearmament under the guise of "police."

In October, the United Nations forces crossed the thirty-eighth parallel and began their march northward. As they reached the bank of the Yalu, the situation assumed serious proportions as a result of the large scale entry into the conflict of Chinese Communist forces.

Against this background, the 9th Session of the Diet opened in November. This was a short session primarily devoted to a revival of old arguments on such issues as neutrality, rearmament, peace, participation in the United Nations, etc. The following are a few of the more characteristic arguments concerning the United Nations: Junzo Sasamori of the Democratic party pressed the government with the question, "How can Japan who has renounced war and is unarmed be qualified for joining the United Nations? How can she perform the duty of taking part in collective sanctions?" Moreover, he suggested that revision of the Constitution would be needed to enable Japan to undertake such obligations. Yoshida evaded answering questions concerning Japan's possible participation in the United Nations. He merely stated: " . . . the Government is not yet in a position to give any answer."[6]

Morio Sasaki, also of the Democratic party, observed: "The time will never come when both worlds will agree to guarantee the security of Japan." He felt "there was no alternative but to rely on the United States."[7] On the other hand, Chozaburo Mizutani

---

5 *Ibid.*, p. 18.

6 *Ibid.*, 9th Sess., No. 4, 25 Nov. 1950, pp. 6-8.

7 Japan, National Diet, Foreign Affairs Ctte. of the House of Representatives, 9th Sess., 25 Nov. 1950 (author's translation).

of the Socialist party argued that "seeking collective security by the United Nations" was "the only way compatible with the Constitution." He felt this course was preferable to "joining either the East or West camps."[8] It is not very clear what he meant by "collective security by the United Nations." The phrase should probably be understood in the sense that collective security should not take the form of affiliation by Japan with one of the two conflicting worlds. But since the United Nations, unlike the League of Nations, acts on the decision-by-majority principle (albeit in modified form), resolutions may well be passed despite the opposition of the minority. Should the opposition minority in the United Nations persist in its own course, in defiance of the majority opinion, other states, out of respect for the principle of decision-by-majority, might have to take sides with "one of the two worlds at strife." It is true that the structure of the United Nations Security Council is based upon the principle of the "unanimity of great powers" which is embodied in the veto power given to the permanent members of the Council. Even so, in some cases, such as the decision to intervene in the Korean War which was taken in the absence of one of the great powers, nations are placed in a dilemma—whether or not to take sides with "one of the two worlds at strife." Collective security on a worldwide scale through the United Nations is not so easy a task as suggested by its advocates, but involves serious problems that have their roots in the nature of the United Nations.

Yoshimori Fukazawa of the Communist party put the matter more succinctly:

> At present the United Nations is being managed in complete disregard of [the spirit of great power agreement], and is going to settle everything merely by a unilateral vote overriding [the] fundamental principle of agreement. . . . As a result . . . it is being managed not as an organization for securing world peace but as a tool to rationalize war.[9]

[8] *Proceedings in the House of Representatives*, 9th Sess., No. 4, 25 Nov. 1950, p. 11.

[9] *Ibid.*, p. 17.

This statement was naturally challenged by the government which answered that it was only proper for Japan to co-operate with the United Nations, because the latter's objective is the maintenance of peace. There certainly is an important question whether the United Nations should perform its security functions on the basis of the principle of the unanimity of the great powers or on the basis of decision-by-majority. But even if military sanctions are decided upon by seven of the eleven members of the Council, including the great powers, localized war will inevitably continue if the nation subject to such sanctions determines on resistance by force. Did Fukazawa mean to reject action in such circumstances as a "rationalization of war"? If so, the United Nations will necessarily be divested of the meaning of its existence, at least insofar as security is concerned. To support the United Nations in its present form, it is necessary first of all to dispel the people's suspicions by completely refuting the Communist criticism and by clarifying the nature and necessity of the measures taken by the United Nations for the maintenance of world peace.

## INITIAL PRESS REACTIONS TO THE KOREAN WAR

At the beginning of the Korean War Japanese press circles entertained some doubts regarding the legal nature of the situation but all expected the United Nations to resort to proper and effective measures for settling the issue. Immediately after the attack on South Korea on 25 June 1950, *Asahi* pointed out that the Republic of Korea had been recognized by the United Nations but that North Korea was recognized by the Soviet Union and Communist China. Each of the Korean governments considered the entire region of the peninsula its territory. Therefore, in the opinion of *Asahi*, the Korean War was, in international law, a civil disturbance and could not be considered an international dispute.

*Yomiuri*, however, maintained that this "civil war" differed from that between the Communist and Nationalist forces in China. In the background was the irrevocable international "cold war" and, therefore, "it could not be said to be a conflict within one nation in the geographical sense of the term." Thus, *Yomiuri* expected the United Nations Security Council to devote itself to the settlement of the situation. *Mainichi* stated that the government of the Republic of Korea was reported to be planning an appeal to the United Nations, and expressed the hope "that an international peace organization such as the United Nations will take positive action." Even *Asahi*, despite its contention that it was difficult to consider the incident an international dispute, said that the substance of the issue called for a political, rather than a legal, approach for its settlement and that the United Nations was expected to assume its supreme duty with regard to a matter so pregnant with profound political consequences.

As soon as the trouble broke out in Korea, the Security Council called upon the North Koreans to stop fighting. *Mainichi* pointed out on 27 June that this decision was taken when the Soviet delegate was absent and there was therefore some doubt as to its legitimacy. But since nine members of the Council supported the resolution, with only Yugoslavia abstaining, the moral effectiveness, if not legal validity, of the resolution could not be negated. On the next day, *Asahi* commented:

> The Soviet Union did not participate in the Security Council decision, but we should consider the fact that it was approved by nine out of eleven Council members. It is not clear what steps may be taken when such a resolution is ignored, but at least the international moral responsibility arising from non-compliance would be extremely serious.

When the North Korean army ignored the Security Council's resolution and continued to move southward, the Council recommended that the member nations "furnish such assistance to the Republic of Korea as may be necessary to repel the armed attack and to restore international peace and security in the area."[10] This in effect meant military intervention by the United Nations in the armed conflict. On 2 July 1950, *Mainichi* commented that, unless this epoch-making decision was carried out with force, "the United Nations, as an agency for the preservation of world peace, would have to commit suicide." According to *Mainichi*, the armed forces of the United States and others were defensive forces in Korea in order to preserve peace under the United Nations, and therefore, the decision to intervene did not mean that at that point the non-Communist nations were going to organize as an international army to wage World War III against the Communist bloc. In other words, the world had not moved from a "cold war" to a "hot war." But the fact that a decision of the United Nations Security Council was being translated into reality with force for the first time meant a vast change in the general situation. This would serve as a strong warning to any nation planning aggression. Furthermore, the action should dispel doubts as to the value of the Security Council. Thus, *Mainichi* observed, "We are very much pleased with the fact that the resolve of the United States and other democratic nations in the United Nations has been so clearly indicated." It expressed firm trust in the United Nations, stating that "it has been made clear what Japan can rely on if it is invaded."

On the basis of a popular sentiment of this same nature, there was a trend toward positive co-operation with the United Nations within the government as well as among the people. This tendency increased day by day, but a warning issued by *Asahi* as early as 4 July 1950 should be noted: "As a matter of principle, there should be a rigorous distinction between the fact that Japan must be obedient to the policy of the Occupation and that Japan volunteers to co-operate with the United States military action in Korea."

Apart from the question of how much co-operation Japan should give the United Nations, the firm actions taken in Korea by the

[10] Security Council, Official Records (S.C.O.R.): 5th Yr., No. 16, 474th Mtg., 27 June 1950, p. 4.

Organization actually gave the Japanese the feeling that they could "rely on the United Nations." It offered tangible proof of the judgment that the United Nations could effectively guarantee Japan's security.

At this juncture, on 9 July, *Asahi* observed:

> The direction the United Nations has followed since the Security Council's recommendation of 25 June shows that the United Nations is automatically changing into a United Nations of non-Communist nations, as ex-President Hoover advocated. And the fact that the organization of a United Nations force under the United Nations flag is being seriously considered by the United States government is extremely significant because of its bearing upon the problems of Japan's security.

The decision of the United Nations was particularly significant for the future handling of international problems because it confirmed the precedent that the absence of a permanent member of the Security Council did not invalidate a decision. This led *Asahi* to re-evaluate the United Nations from the viewpoint of Japan's security.

> On the basis of this development, the United Nations can even assume the task of safeguarding Japan. . . . It may be said that the chances for settling the security issue which has been hampering the conclusion of a peace treaty have been increased considerably.

As everyone knows, the quick, decisive action by the United Nations was the result of the mighty driving force of the United States. Even though the United Nations action in Korea was actually based primarily on United States strength, it is impossible to overlook the fact that there is a fundamental difference between action based on a United Nations decision and action which is not. In an article in *Asahi* on 13 July, Professor Kisaburo Yokota emphasized this point:

> The fact that the United Nations took quick and effective action with regard to the Korean War offers a valuable

> suggestion for the future security of Japan. As is well known, the actual military action was almost entirely that of the United States. But the action was taken through the United Nations, which in turn gave it international prestige. Therefore, the action was all the more effective and endowed with all the more prestige.

The sense of trust in the United Nations rapidly rose with the outbreak of the Korean War and found expression in the insistence that Japan should co-operate as fully as possible with the United Nations action. In Prime Minister Yoshida's speech of 15 July to the emergency session of the Diet, he stated that the United Nations action in Korea had boosted Japan's faith in the O.ganization and that Japan would co-operate with the United Nations "within the limits of her ability."[11] This statement demonstrated that Japan, faced with the menace of Communist force, hoped to clarify its international position by joining with the other free nations to contribute to world peace.

*Yomiuri* commented on this statement as follows:

> The United Nations action which met aggression with force is the only guarantee of security for unarmed Japan.
>
> It is a matter of course that we should give all possible co-operation to the United Nations in its action. . . . It is nonsense in the world of today to emphasize universal peace and permanent neutrality. . . . Although we wish for harmony between the two worlds, we should not confuse mere wishes with reality.

A similar view was expressed by Professor Tomoo Otaka in an article in the 16 July issue of *Yomiuri:*

> With the world divided in two, there are those who insist that Japan should become a bridge between the two worlds. But this way of thinking is too far removed from actuality; it is too presumptuous an idealism.

[11] *Proceedings in the House of Representatives*, 8th Sess., No. 3, 14 July 1950, p. 2.

Dr. Hideki Yukawa, world-famed professor of physics, also felt that Japan should seek security through the United Nations. Writing in *Mainichi* on 31 July, he stated:

> It seems to me that the only right way for Japan is to seek for peace and security through the United Nations. The United Nations prompt action at the outbreak of the Korean War proved that the ideal of Japan—to have its security guaranteed by the United Nations—was not an idle dream.

## ATTITUDE OF THE LABOR UNIONS

General approval of the use of force by the United Nations in the Korean War and of Japan's co-operating with this move was indicated by leaders of non-Communist-affiliated labor unions. For instance, Zengoro Shimagami of the General Council of Labor Unions (*Sohyo*), who is also a member of the Left Wing Socialist party, observed in an article in *Yomiuri* on 17 August:

> The Japan Communist party and the labor unions affiliated with it (including *Zenroren*, the All-Japan Labor Union League) are clearly supporting the North Koreans. They say this is a war for the liberation of the South Korean people. To them, a war started by North Korea is a war of liberation, and the United Nations forces are interfering in domestic matters. This is a highly convenient argument. . . . The military action, which is a police action by the United Nations, taken because North Korea did not abide by the decision of the United Nations Security Council, must be approved so long as it remains within the limits of the United Nations decision. . . .
>
> Now the question is how should labor unions act? It was inevitable that the Communist-affiliated *Zenroren* and the democratic labor unions affiliated with *Sohyo* would take clearly divergent actions. *Zenroren*, which supports North Korea, is against "special procurement" production and transportation which are intended for use against the North Koreans. . . . But we intend to support these measures. This

is not a subservient attitude based on the fact that such a course is inevitable because Japan is under occupation. And if we were to pursue this policy as a "purely economic" action to receive wages, it would be insulting the workers. We do it because we support the United Nations police action.

## ATTITUDES OF THE POLITICAL PARTIES ON CO-OPERATION WITH THE UNITED NATIONS

The question whether and how Japan should co-operate with the United Nations action in Korea continued to be the subject of much discussion and in early September the newspaper *Mainichi* sought the views of the Liberal, Democratic, and Socialist parties on the subject, "How would you co-operate with the United Nations?" The six questions raised by *Mainichi* were discussed by the official organs of the parties; their written replies, which may be considered "the official replies from the parties," were published on 10 September 1950:

Q. 1: Do you approve of the action taken by the United Nations regarding Korea?

All three parties "approved."

Q. 2: If you approve of the United Nations action, what attitude do you think Japan should take?

*Liberal party:* Japan should give the maximum co-operation permitted.

*Democratic party:* Overall co-operation within the limits of the spirit of the Constitution and the policy of the Army of Occupation.

*Socialist party:* Since Japan is under military occupation, this is no time for the state and government to express an official attitude; but the people should support the United Nations decision within the framework of the Constitution.

Q. 3: If you support co-operation with the United Nations, which of the following specific steps do you think Japan should take?: (a) spiritual co-operation; (b) responding to the United Nations demand for production and transportation as required by military operations; (c) developing a great national movement for co-operation with the United Nations?

*Liberal party:*

(a) Naturally.

(b) We should not impair the United Nations action but give positive and overall co-operation.

(c) We expect the people will co-operate spontaneously.

*Democratic party:*

(a) No.

(b) Japan's response should not be limited in scope to what the United Nations demands.

(c) Japan should give positive and overall co-operation.

*Socialist party:*

(a) We abide by the spirit of repelling aggressors and maintaining peace and order, and this does not mean that we do not translate spirit into action.

(b) It is natural that Japan should co-operate with the United Nations.

(c) Because of the Constitution, overall co-operation which includes taking up arms is impossible; but we should start a national peace movement to support the United Nations efforts to prevent war and establish peace.

Q. 4: Would you co-operate with the United Nations unconditionally, even if the United Nations forces cross the thirty-eighth parallel in the future?

*Liberal party:* Our attitude of co-operation with the United Nations will not change.

*Democratic party:* We will co-operate.

*Socialist party:* We cannot answer hypothetical questions.

Q. 5: If the United Nations demanded that Japan offer military bases, would you respond favorably?

*Liberal party:* We should like to avoid hypothetical arguments, but we are convinced that as a matter of sentiment we should consent.

*Democratic party:* There is nothing wrong with consenting.

*Socialist party:* We are against offering military bases to either of the two opposing great power blocs. But we would have to give the matter thought if the United Nations should demand bases as a condition for shouldering the guarantee of Japan's security.

Q. 6: Granting the understandable popular preference for avoiding getting involved in war and maintaining neutrality, how can Japan realize these objectives and maintain co-operation with the United Nations?

*Liberal party:* We appreciate the popular feelings, but they are due to a lack of understanding of the world situation. The people do not know the horrors of a Communist state. "Peace movement" is a euphonious name but it serves the interests of the Communist states.

*Democratic party:* As a practical matter, the maintenance of neutrality is difficult in view of the geographical position of our country and the world situation.

*Socialist party:* When a war of aggression disturbs justice and order, there can be no isolationism. We should support the United Nations efforts to maintain order and prevent war. The non-military neutrality stated in the Constitution is possible only so long as the United Nations is sound.

According to this survey by *Mainichi*, not only the conservative Liberal and Democratic parties but also the progressive Socialist party expressed a policy of positive support for the United Nations, thus measurably negating its previous standoffish, neutralistic position.

## THE IMPASSE IN THE UNITED NATIONS

The sudden surge of trust in the United Nations after the outbreak of the Korean War was expressed by *Mainichi* in its editorial on 19 September 1950, in the following terms: "The attitude of the Japanese people toward the United Nations has been already determined by the Korean War." But later Japanese public opinion, reacting sharply to the progress of the Korean War and the steps taken by the United Nations, reflected some degree of vacillation and skepticism in its trust in the United Nations. This was not due to temporary phenomena, such as the United Nations forces coming face to face with the peril of intervention by Chinese Communist forces, but to the fact that the United Nations, which had acted so firmly and quickly against the action of the North Korean army, was unable to make up its mind what to do when the Chinese Communists entered the war. This appeared to be a sign of inconsistency which gave rise to doubts about devotion to the principles of the United Nations.

The Soviet delegation to the United Nations ended its boycott of the Security Council in August 1950. According to an analysis printed in *Asahi* on 29 July 1950, the Soviet Union recognized the effectiveness of the United Nations for its own foreign policy purposes, and found it could not easily abandon the world organization as a propaganda instrument. By boycotting this important agency, the Soviet Union had created a situation disadvantageous to its own interests. Although the Soviet Union denounced the Security Council decision as illegal, this argument was without force since the Soviet delegate had not attended the Council meeting. As long as the Soviet Union did not withdraw from the United Nations, there was no alternative for it but to return to the United Nations. In returning, the Soviet Union was attempting to do what it had tried to do earlier by boycotting the Organization. Even though the methods differed, the purpose was the same insofar as the intention of expanding the strength of international communism was concerned. Furthermore, after returning to the Security Council, the Soviet delegate became President of the Council and was able from this position to maneuver for advantage. One of his first acts was to rule that the delegate of Nationalist China should not be seated at the Council table because he did not represent China. But the Soviet delegate was overruled by a vote of eight to three because the United Kingdom and Norway, both of which recognize Communist China, voted against the Soviet ruling.[12]

Commenting on this development, *Yomiuri* stated on 3 August, "One of the important objectives of the Soviet Union in returning to the Security Council has already come to naught." But the Soviet Union would never give up the desire of bringing Communist China into the United Nations. The Soviet Union, it would seem, will remain in the world organization even after failing to get Communist China admitted to membership and continue to "follow the policy of making utmost use of the arena of the United Nations."

After assuming the presidency of the Security Council, the Soviet delegate attempted to justify the action of the North Korean army. The Council became a propaganda arena and could not discharge its responsibilities in dealing with problems such as the Korean issue which required quick action. It was under these circumstances that the fifth session of the General Assembly convened on 19 September 1950. *Asahi* expected much from the Assembly and observed that it could act by a two-thirds majority and could "contribute greatly to the settlement of the situation." According to its editorial of 19 September, if the Security Council decision, taken while the Soviet delegate was absent, were to be approved by the General Assembly, the Soviet protest would lose its power and the United Nations action would be justified. Such an event would produce a great psychological effect, for although a recommendation by the General Assembly may not have the same power as a decision by the Security Council, "a decision adopted by a majority at a 'town

---

[12] S.C.O.R., 5th Yr., No. 22, 480th Mtg., 1 Aug. 1950, pp. 1-9.

meeting' of the world, attended by the delegates from 59 nations . . . would doubtless influence world public opinion tremendously."

As a matter of fact, there were plans within the United Nations for strengthening the General Assembly. The Assembly approved the Acheson plan which set forth procedures for quickly calling an emergency session of the Assembly to meet urgent problems, and established a Peace Observation Commission to guard against aggression. *Asahi*, welcoming these moves toward strengthening the General Assembly, observed on 22 October:

> Thus, the United Nations which, it was once feared, might reach an impasse because of the abuse of the veto by the Soviet Union, has developed into a worldwide security system which, unlike the League of Nations, has genuine strength and it has started a mighty forward move toward endowing the world with a bright future.

Despite this move to strengthen the General Assembly, the Japanese press continued to express its concern over the weakness of the Organization, particularly the veto-ridden Security Council. With the return of the Soviet delegate, it was apparent that the Security Council would again fall into a state of paralysis. Insofar as effective steps against aggression were within the exclusive power of the Security Council, the sense of trust in security through the United Nations was shaken. This was a natural conclusion for those who considered directly associating the United Nations with "Japan's security."

*Yomiuri* referred to this kind of uneasiness on 21 September 1950 and pointed out that "under the present circumstances where the veto is recognized in the Security Council, guarantees provided by the United Nations are by no means sufficient for the security of Japan." To consider the United Nations from the standpoint of Japanese security, it is necessary to go beyond theoretical and general considerations. As the *Yomiuri* editorial of 24 October stated it: "It is our duty to consider the tasks of the United Nations as problems of life and death which have a direct bearing upon Japan's international position."

One issue that was repeatedly brought up in the discussion about the United Nations was the veto system. The principle of great power agreement was one of the bases on which the United Nations was founded. It was believed that through this principle the United Nations would become a powerful security organization. One manifestation of this fundamental principle was the veto right given to the great powers but it was the use of this veto which betrayed the idea of the United Nations as a strong security organization. As a result the prospect of security through the United Nations was seriously weakened. *Asahi* observed on 26 October 1950 that there was a basic problem "in the fact that no rules were laid down to meet the situation when one of the big five powers resorted to aggression." Were the United Nations to take measures against a great power engaged in an act of aggression, it would mean that the Organization was "provoking" rather than "preventing" war. Thus, although the veto is still a canker of the United Nations, it nonetheless prevents the Organization from engaging in a major war. Yet this "United Nations with the veto" cannot be considered an organization on which states, especially the small nations, can depend.

## COMMUNIST CHINA'S INTERVENTION IN KOREA

The United Nations forces, on reaching the bank of the Yalu River on 4 November 1950, confirmed the fact that Chinese Communist forces were already engaged in the Korean War. At this same time Communist China announced that its "volunteers" were participating in the war in aid of North Korea. General MacArthur, Commander of the United Nations Forces, said, " . . . we face an entirely new war. This has shattered the high hopes we entertained that . . . the war in Korea could be brought to a rapid close. . . ."[13] It goes without saying that quick action by the United Nations to deal with this new situation was called for. An *Asahi* editorial of 30 November stated, "The United Nations must quickly find a road to peace through a political solution." And *Mainichi* remarked, "For alleviating and solving the existing crisis, great hope is placed on the role of the United Nations."

But now that the Chinese Communists had intervened in the Korean War, varying nuances in the attitude of the great powers in the United Nations (other than the Soviet Union) inevitably began to emerge. While the United States pressed for a "general offensive," the United Kingdom desired "negotiations," which indicated that these two powers did not always see eye to eye. At this time (1 December) President Truman expressed the resolve that necessary steps would be taken to accomplish the mission of the United Nations forces in Korea.[14] Concerning this *Mainichi* observed on 6 December:

> If the United Nations forces were to give in out of fear of the Chinese intervention, the nations which had placed their hopes on the ability of the United Nations to preserve peace in the world would again be thrown into a state of disappointment and insecurity. It is just and proper that the United States President expressed resolve at this vital moment.

*Yomiuri* commented on 10 December that whether or not the hopes for peace would be realized depended solely upon the attitude of Communist China and went on to state, "If it becomes clear that Communist China does not desire peace, the Western world should not hesitate to take powerful measures in concert through the United Nations in order to live up to the principles of the United Nations Charter."

---

[13] *The New York Times*, 29 Nov. 1950. Cited in U.S. Senate, 82nd Cong., 1st Sess., *Hearings before the Ctte. on Armed Services and the Ctte. on Foreign Relations on Military Situation in the Far East*, p. 3495.

[14] U.S. Dept. of State *Bulletin*, Vol. XXIII, No. 597 (11 Dec. 1950), pp. 925-28.

Although the firm resolve of the United States was clearly indicated, the bemuddled and irresolute attitude of the United Nations itself was carried over to the next year. In the light of this situation, press circles in Japan began criticizing the United Nations. They raised the question whether the United Nations attitude toward a great power differed from that toward a small power. *Asahi* commented on 7 January 1951:

> The United Nations adjudged that North Korea was an aggressor within less than three days and resorted to military action. Now it is ten days since the Chinese Communist army started a far larger operation than that originally undertaken by the North Korean Army. The thirty-eighth parallel has again been crossed, but the United Nations is still watching the situation without taking action. The Political Committee is not yet ready to declare Communist China an aggressor. As long as the Western European states do not agree on united action regarding Communist China, the latter may decide to behave as it desires in Korea. . . . The Chinese Communist army intervened in the Korean War under the pretext of aiding North Korea and defending its own land. But the United Nations did not even advise its withdrawal. The only thing the United Nations could do was to propose a cease-fire. The failure to declare Communist China . . . an aggressor is perhaps due to preparations for peaceful diplomatic negotiations. But if a decision is not made, will it not affect the prestige of the United Nations in the event that negotiations bog down? . . . If the acts of a small power are condemned but not those of a big power, the world would eventually be ruled by sheer force. . . .

The Chinese Communist government rejected the proposal by the United Nations Political Committee for a cease-fire to be followed by negotiations on other issues; it stuck to the policy of continuing hostilities and making the settlement of various Asian problems a condition for a cease-fire. It became clear that Communist China intended to sell the cease-fire the United Nations sought at the highest possible price. This forced the United Nations to assume a clear-cut attitude and finally the General Assembly, on 1 February, by a vote of 44 to 7 with 9 abstentions, approved the United States proposal charging the People's Republic of China with engaging in aggression in Korea.[15] The next day *Asahi* commented:

> The North Korean government was branded an aggressor by the United Nations within a few days after embarking upon aggression, and military action to back up this denunciation was taken by means of the United Nations forces. It was rather illogical that Communist China which entered the Korean War in November of last year and has been engaged in open hostilities against the United Nations forces should not yet have been treated as an aggressor. This is a matter which affects the prestige and destiny of the United Nations and reminds us of the fact that the League of Nations lost its prestige and *raison d'être* as a world peace organization when it failed to deal with acts of aggression. We presume that the United Nations acted cautiously in pursuing a practical policy of preserving peace in the world because the nation to be dealt with this time was Communist China, one of the great powers of the world, and one which has the backing of the Soviet Union. In such circumstances, the matter could not be disposed of by logic alone. But now the proposal for condemning Communist China has been approved. The United Nations action now has been made consistent.

---

[15] See General Assembly Resolution 498(V), 1 Feb. 1951 and G.A.O.R., 5th Sess., 327th Plenary Mtg., 1 Feb. 1951, p. 696.

*chapter five*

# The Fourth Period: The Peace Treaty and the Security Treaty

(February 1951—February 1953)

As pointed out in the previous chapter, with the vigorous steps taken by the United Nations at the outbreak of the Korean War, the people of Japan were struck with a feeling of confidence in the United Nations. At the same time scepticism concerning the United Nations increased among those who adhered to the creed of absolute pacifism. On the basis of these conflicting attitudes, two different views developed concerning the peace treaty which was to terminate the occupation of Japan. In one group were the people who considered that Japan should first seek the conclusion of peace negotiations with a community of liberal states. It was felt to be a sheer impossibility for Japan to shake hands simultaneously and on equal terms with the two worlds which were involved in such large scale opposition and strife. On the other hand, there were those who insisted upon peace with all nations, arguing that for Japan to conclude a peace treaty with one of the conflicting worlds would not only alienate the other, but might also involve Japan in a future war. Of course, all shared the hope that the opposition between the two worlds would be mitigated so that peace with all nations could be realized. However, it was recognized that mere hopes and ideals could not render impossibilities possible.

## PRELIMINARY DISCUSSIONS IN THE DIET

At the 10th Session of the Diet, which opened early in 1951, a matter of the greatest consequence for Japan was discussed: the negotiation of a peace treaty and methods for insuring Japan's security after the conclusion of a treaty. The Cabinet, supported by the Liberal party, took the middle course between the Democrats with their increasing emphasis upon rearmament and the Socialists with their neutral leanings for "peace on a world-wide basis." The government opposed rearmament on the one hand, and tended to support "peace with the majority" on the other.

Yoshida, in his speech on 26 January 1951 in the Diet, gave strong warning to the advocates of rearmament: "Our discussions on rearmament have already caused needless misgivings at home and abroad, and moreover . . . any adequate rearming is an economic impossibility for defeated Japan."[1] Once the government rejected opinions in favor of neutrality and peace on a world-wide scale as being unrealistic, it was necessary to devise some other concrete plan for Japan's security after the conclusion of peace. At this point, John Foster Dulles came to Japan as a special envoy of the United States. Yoshida, on the basis of his talks with Dulles, made the following report in the House of Councillors on 13 February:

> Under the present strained international circumstances, none of the countries in the world would be able to guarantee its

[1] Japan, National Diet, *Official Gazette Extra* (English edition), *Minutes of Proceedings in the House of Councillors*, 10th Sess., No. 4, 26 Jan. 1951, p. 5. Hereinafter referred to as *Proceedings in the House of Councillors.*

> security singlehanded . . . against the aggression of communism. . . . Mr. Dulles indicated that America is prepared to give Japan armed assistance if she [Japan] so desires . . . to repulse aggression . . . against her. I trust that to enter into such operative relations with America is the most appropriate measure under the present international circumstances, which would be welcomed by the majority of the people.[2]

Thus, Japan's policy of returning to the international community by means of a peace treaty with the majority of the nations and by means of the Japanese-American Security Treaty may be said to have been tentatively decided.

The reason that a regional security program such as the Japanese-American Security Treaty began to take concrete shape was that the admission of Japan to the United Nations was beyond prediction and, furthermore, it was not considered that even if this occurred, Japan's security would be sufficiently ensured. The government, of course, repeatedly expressed the view that even non-members of the United Nations might come within the United Nations security system. This view was stated briefly by Kumao Nishimura, a government member of the Foreign Affairs Committee in the 10th Session of the Diet. He said:

> The United Nations' clear objectives of international peace and security would be difficult to attain if the provisions for security are restricted to members of the United Nations. . . . It is, therefore, not too much to conclude that the non-members of the United Nations are also entitled to these benefits.[3]

Whether the safety of a specific nation can be perfectly ensured by the "general security" offered by the United Nations, was, in Nishimura's opinion, a political rather than a legal question. It is

---

[2] *Ibid.*, No. 13, 13 Feb. 1951, p. 3.

[3] Japan, National Diet, Foreign Affairs Ctte. of the House of Representatives, 10th Sess., 14 March 1951 (author's translation).

a matter for each individual nation to decide in consideration of various situations. Article 51 of the Charter permits each nation to take, at least initially, such measures as it deems fit to repel an armed attack, and also establishes the right of collective self-defense. This may be said to provide a theoretical basis for the idea that a special agreement such as the Japanese-American Security Treaty is in no way contradictory to the "general security" system of the United Nations.

The 11th Session of the Diet (August 1951) was convened for the purpose of selecting the Japanese delegates to sign the Peace Treaty. As the session lasted for just three days, only general topics were brought up for discussion. Briefly, the views of the principal parties concerning the Peace Treaty and the Japanese-American Security Treaty were as follows:

(1) The Liberal party supported both treaties and was alive to the necessity of the security agreement, pending Japan's admission to the United Nations.

(2) The Democratic party was also in favor of both instruments provided the conditions were acceptable; the party emphatically supported rearmament and positive participation in the United Nations.

(3) The Right Wing Socialists supported the Peace Treaty, but were antagonistic to the Security Treaty.

(4) The Left Wing Socialists opposed both treaties.

(5) The Workers and Farmers party, from its standpoint of absolute neutralism, made scathing comments on Japan's establishing a connection with a particular state on the pretext of "security." It was felt that this would involve Japan in international complications.

(6) The Communist party opposed both the Peace Treaty and the Security Treaty and was furthermore against Japan's participation in the United Nations.

## CONCLUSION OF THE PEACE TREATY AND THE SECURITY TREATY

On 4 September 1951 the delegates of a number of nations which had joined in the war against Japan assembled for a conference to conclude a Peace Treaty with Japan. The conference met under the chairmanship of the United States Secretary of State, Dean Acheson, in the Opera House in San Francisco, where six years previously, another conference had been held for the establishment of the United Nations. The conference opened with an explanation of the draft treaty given by the United States delegate, John Foster Dulles. This was followed by statements by the delegates of other nations. Amendments introduced by the Soviet delegate, Andrei Gromyko, met with opposition from the majority of delegates, who supported the original draft. Shigeru Yoshida, the chief Japanese delegate, stated: "We are willing to accept this Peace Treaty."

On 8 September the treaty was signed by the delegates of forty-nine nations: Argentina, Australia, Belgium, Bolivia, Brazil, Cambodia, Canada, Ceylon, Chile, Colombia, Costa Rica, Cuba, Dominican Republic, Ecuador, Egypt, El Salvador, Ethiopia, France, Greece, Guatemala, Haiti, Honduras, Indonesia, Iran, Iraq, Laos, Lebanon, Liberia, Luxembourg, Mexico, the Netherlands, New Zealand, Nicaragua, Norway, Pakistan, Panama, Paraguay, Peru, Philippines, Saudi Arabia, Syria, Turkey, the Union of South Africa, the United Kingdom, the United States, Uruguay, Venezuela, Vietnam, and Japan. Simultaneously with this Peace Treaty, the Japanese-American Security Treaty was concluded.

In October the 12th Session of the Japanese Diet met to ratify both treaties. Yoshida's speech on that occasion may be said to have been the final judgment of the government and the party in power on the issues raised in the previous debates in the Diet:

> Chapter III [of the Peace Treaty] . . . stipulates Japan's acceptance of . . . Article 2 of the United Nations Charter and the confirmation by the Allied Powers that they will

> also be guided by the same principles in their relations with Japan. Such a stipulation would be unnecessary if Japan were to be permitted to join the United Nations forthwith upon her recovery of independence. However, in the light of the fact that many qualified nations are being denied admission through the exercise of veto by big Powers, I should like to call your attention to the importance of the relations Japan is to maintain with Allied nations in regard to the matter of security. . . . It is also explicitly recognized that Japan as a sovereign nation possesses the inherent right of individual or collective self-defense referred to in Article 51 of the Charter of the United Nations, and that Japan may voluntarily enter into collective security arrangements.[4]

In regard to the basis and nature of the Japanese-American Security Treaty, Nobuyuki Okuma, chairman of the Special Committee for the Treaty of Peace and the Security Treaty in the House of Councillors, made a report indicating the government's intention:

> As there is still irresponsible aggression in the world, it is the current international conception to organize collective security, and it is absolutely necessary to resort to this . . . security to protect the country, which has no armament, on the recovery of independence and freedom. This is necessary for its own defence, for the peace of the Far East and of the world. According to government explanations, this is the reason for which the security treaty was signed.[5]

Japan, needless to say, wished to contribute to peace through the United Nations, but it was recognized that it might be many years before Japan would be allowed to join the United Nations. This accounted for the conclusion of the Security Treaty. According to the government's interpretation, "The Security Treaty has been concluded as a stopgap measure to cover the period prior to our admission into the United Nations."[6]

---

[4] *Proceedings in the House of Councillors,* 12th Sess., No. 3, 12 Oct. 1951, p. 3.

[5] *Ibid.*, No. 20, 18 Nov. 1951, p. 2.

[6] *Ibid.*, p. 10.

The government's policy quite naturally met with scathing denunciation from those opposition parties which were against both treaties. Makoto Hori of the Workers and Farmers party, for example, said, "These two Treaties will place Japan internationally in a new subordinate relation." He felt that there were great possibilities of Japan's being involved in war and that the two treaties would only serve "to aggravate the existing world situation."[7] The Communists contended that these pacts offered to the American troops Japan's total "manpower and material resources" and that they meant "the sale of the sovereignty and independence of Japan."[8] The majority of members of the Diet, however, supported and approved the treaties and with increasing vigor demanded the admission of Japan to the United Nations.

In the same session of the Diet, the question arose as to how Japan, having renounced armament and the right to wage war, could, as stated in the Peace Treaty, accept the obligations set forth in Article 2 of the United Nations Charter. How could Japan discharge the obligation "to give the United Nations every assistance in any action taken under the Charter"? The government's reply was as follows:

> The treaty obligation of Japan is satisfied if . . . she gives "the United Nations every assistance in any action it takes in accordance with the Charter" on the decision of the Security Council and within limits of Japanese law.[9]

That is to say, such assistance should be given insofar as the national power and legal system of Japan permits.

On 28 April 1952 the Treaty of Peace came into effect and Japan was restored to its former position as a regular member of the international community. However, peace still remained unrestored between Japan on the one hand and the Soviet Union and Communist

---

[7] *Ibid.*, p. 26.
[8] *Ibid.*, p. 28.
[9] *Ibid.*, p. 4.

China on the other. In the 13th Session of the Diet, which lasted from 11 December 1951 to 31 July 1952, Yoshida stated: "We desire to obtain a seat quickly in the United Nations. But even prior to our admission into that organization we will continue to cooperate whole-heartedly in all U.N. measures for peace."[10] The government, while stating its opposition to rearmament, recognized the need for self-defense and adopted a policy of "gradual increase in the power of self-defense." The Socialists, who opposed this policy, nevertheless supported the United Nations and regional collective security. Chozaburo Mizutani, a Right Wing Socialist representative, for example, spoke as follows:

> We support the United Nations as [the] sole existing organ for the world peace. We have to correct its defects and . . . strengthen its function for international security so as to eventually disarm all of the countries in the world . . . [We] admit, under the present situation of the world, the right of collective self-defence and the system of regional security as provided in [Article] 51 of the United Nations Charter within the scope of the Constitution . . .[11]

## DIET DISCUSSION ON THE UNITED NATIONS

The 13th Session of the Diet was marked by detailed questions and answers about various problems relating to the United Nations. In the meetings of the Foreign Affairs Committees in each House, Katsuo Okazaki, Foreign Minister, and Kumao Nishimura, Chief of the Treaty Bureau of the Foreign Ministry, took it upon themselves to answer on behalf of the government. The tenor of their answers was often only a confirmation of government statements which have already been quoted in this study. However, in order to elucidate the attitude of the Japanese government on major

---

[10] *Ibid.*, 13th Sess., No. 5, 23 Jan. 1952, p. 7.

[11] *Ibid.*, No. 7, 25 Jan. 1952, p. 8.

problems regarding the United Nations, these questions and the government's replies are here summarized.

*Disarmament and UN Membership:* Etsujiro Uehara of the Liberal party raised the question of Japan's disarmament. He pointed out that as the United Nations has for its objective the attainment of the security of the world by collective action, Japan upon joining the United Nations will have a duty to perform in this connection. In order to perform it, it is only right that Japan should have armaments worthy of a member of the United Nations. He asked for the government's opinion on this matter.

Hanji Ogawa of the Democratic party raised a similar question: In the light of the Charter, in particular, Articles 43, 45, and others, is not the ability of a state to defend its territory by its own forces a qualification for membership in the United Nations? *In fine*, is not armament a pre-condition necessary for admission to the United Nations?

The government replied to these questions as follows: The matter of rearmament is totally separate from the question of seeking admission to the United Nations. It is the objective of the United Nations to build a world where even unarmed nations can live in safety. To make armaments a prerequisite of admission to the United Nations would be inconsistent with the spirit of the Organization. The terms of admission as set out in Article 4 of the Charter do not mention any duty concerning armament. The only question that arises concerns Article 2, paragraph 5, of the Charter, with its provision that all members of the United Nations should give the United Nations every assistance in any action it takes in accordance with the Charter. The said provisions are recognized as incompatible with the position of a nation which stands on the principle of permanent neutrality. The word "assistance" in the case of armed nations naturally involves assistance by military forces, but other nations are capable of discharging their duties as prescribed in the Charter by giving other types of assistance to the United Nations. Any state, even if unarmed, is able to perform the duty prescribed in the Charter by giving assistance such as approval of the passage through its territory of United Nations forces, the offer of bases, and the supply of goods. In other words, the state concerned has only to provide aid insofar as it does not run counter to its national law. The lack of armaments is thus no obstacle to admission to the United Nations.

There are few nations in the world that are capable of defending their lands by their own forces alone. This provides the reason for the system of "collective security." Aside from the practical question whether a state is capable of providing for its own defense, as a matter of principle any state, so long as it remains independent and is capable of providing for its own defense, should properly have the intention and ability to defend its territory by its own force. Under the Japanese-American Security Treaty, the United States expects a gradual increase in Japan's power of self-defense. It is inevitable under the existing Constitution, however illogical it may seem, that a country like Japan, which plays a role of considerable proportion in the world in economic and other matters, should be totally lacking in the power of national defense. From a legal point of view alone, the possession of military forces is not a necessary condition for membership of the United Nations. We have the examples of Panama and Costa Rica, nations without armaments, which were among the original members of the United Nations. Later, Iceland obtained admission despite its declared disarmament. This precedent may be applied, as a matter of principle, to Japan.

*Admission and the Veto:* The issue of the use of the veto on membership applications was raised by Naokichi Kitamura of the Liberal party. He observed that Italy's application for admission to the United Nations was turned down in the Security Council owing to the exercise of the veto by the Soviet Union. He also mentioned the Soviet veto of the application of Jordan on the ground that foreign forces were stationed in that country. Considering that United States forces were to be stationed in Japan in accordance with the Japanese-American Security Treaty, he asked whether there was not considerable likelihood that Japan's application for admission would eventually be rejected in the Security Council owing to Soviet obstruction?

The government's reply was: The stationing of foreign forces in Japan neither signifies an incapacity to accept the obligations provided for in the Charter nor proves an obstacle to admission to the United Nations. It is true that the Soviet Union had some doubts about the qualifications of Jordan as an independent state because of the stationing of British forces there. This view, however, has been opposed by other states, particularly in Western Europe. Success or failure of an application for admission to the United Nations is not predictable before the application is actually made. So long as the measures Japan takes are proper, even if there should be a fear of a Soviet veto, application for admission should be made. The government intended to do so, even though it was not sure of success.

Satoko Togano of the Socialist party also touched on this issue: Is there not an atmosphere of uncertainty in the United Nations Security Council and the General Assembly over what is to be done about the fact that the veto has kept a number of states out of the Organization?

The government admitted that this was a controversial problem. It was not wise that the application of any state for admission to the United Nations should be referred initially to the Security Council because of all the possibilities of rejection through the exercise of the veto by some great power. With regard to serious questions concerning the use of military force, the veto can properly be exercised by a great power; but the veto should not apply to the admission of new members to the United Nations. Many members of the Organization have supported this view. Though some consider that there should be an amendment to the Charter so that the General Assembly would decide on the admission of new members, this change remains unrealized because any revision of the Charter requires the agreement of the great powers. On the other hand, the difficulty is all the more aggravated because of the recent rumor of a proposal by the Soviet Union to the effect that in return for admission of Italy and other states, which had been denied admission by the exercise of the Soviet veto, nations in the Communist bloc should also obtain admission. However, some members of the United Nations asserted that this proposal was too opportunistic and did not comply with the principles of the Charter.

*Position of Non-Members of the United Nations:* Satoko Togano drew attention to Article 35 of the Charter which provides that even a non-member of the United Nations is entitled to bring any dispute to which it is a party to the attention of the Security Council or the General Assembly. Since non-members do not bear any part of the expenses of the Organization, how then can they demand action from the United Nations?

The government's answer was that the major objective of the United Nations was the preservation of international peace and security. This can be attained through intimate relationships not only among the members of the United Nations but also among non-members. This accounts for the provision in Article 35 of the Charter that even a non-member of the United Nations is qualified to bring to the attention of the Security Council or the General Assembly any dispute to which it is a party. So far as making use of the Organization for the preservation of international peace and security is concerned, the non-members of the United Nations are practically on an equal footing with members.

*Associate Membership:* If the early admission to the United Nations which Japan ardently hoped for was difficult to realize, Yoshio Namiki of the Democratic party asked, should not some alternative such as associate membership be considered? Could not Japanese observers be attached to the United Nations?

The government's attitude toward this suggestion was that the United Nations system does not provide for associate membership, but with the approval of the Secretary-General, observers can be sent. This was a step the government wished to take as quickly as possible.

*Permanent Neutrality:* Was there any truth in, or reason for, the opinion that membership in the United Nations was incompatible with permanent neutrality, asked Mr. Namiki.

The government spokesman drew attention to the fact that at the San Francisco Conference on the drafting of the United Nations Charter, there was a French proposal that some phrase should be included in the Charter providing that no nation could adopt a status of neutrality with the object of evading its duties as specified in the Charter. By "status of neutrality" was meant the position of permanent neutrality. The interpretation agreed upon at the Conference, however, implied that any nation adopting this position of permanent neutrality was not released from the obligations stipulated in the Charter. It was decided, therefore, that there would be no particular necessity for adopting the French proposal.[12] Switzerland, though once a member of the League of Nations, was not a member of the United Nations. In principle, the United Nations and permanent neutrality are deemed incompatible.

*The Japanese-American Security Treaty:* Mr. Namiki also queried whether, in the event of Japan obtaining admission to the United Nations, there would be any need for the Japanese-American Security Treaty.

The government pointed out that the Charter permits regional arrangements. The North Atlantic Treaty was actually concluded in accordance with such provisions. Even if Japan should be admitted to the United Nations, the Security Treaty would presumably be effective. In fact, such a pact would be rendered all the more desirable so far as the United Nations is concerned.

*The Korean War:* Hisao Kuroda of the Workers and Farmers party raised the issue of the legality of United Nations action in

---

[12] See *Documents of the United Nations Conference on International Organization, San Francisco, 1945* (New York: United Nations Information Organizations, 1945), Vol. III, p. 383, and Vol. VI, pp. 400-01.

Korea. He pointed out that "the special agreements" provided for in Article 43 of the Charter had not yet been concluded, so military actions could not be taken in accordance with Article 42. Thus, in the case of the Korean War, the dispatch of the United Nations forces was not based upon Articles 42 and 43 of the Charter. He asked, on what authority then was this action based?

The government stated that the action resulted from a recommendation made in accordance with Article 39 of the Charter.

This issue was also raised by Hyakuro Hayashi of the Communist party with a view to demonstrating the illegality of the United Nations military actions.

He posed two questions: Granting that the present military action in Korea is outside the scope of Article 42 of the Charter, in what sense is this "action" provided for in the first part of Article 39? He also asked whether it was not contrary to the Charter that air, naval, and ground forces were in action in the name of the United Nations apparently in accordance with Article 42, but actually based upon Article 39 of the Charter.

The government's reply was as follows: These questions arise from Mr. Hayashi's lack of knowledge of the past. It is true that action under Article 42 would have been justified in the Korean situation. However, this was impossible for two reasons: firstly, the principle of unanimous agreement among the Big Five had paralyzed the effective functioning of the Security Council; secondly, the carrying out of military measures as provided for in Article 42 presupposed the conclusion of "special agreements" as specified in Article 43. The present state of affairs, in which no such arrangements existed, made it impossible to put Articles 42 and 43 of the Charter into practical operation. This was the reason for the threatened peace and security of the world today, as Mr. Hayashi must know better than anybody else. At the outbreak of the Korean War, a number of nations were well aware that, as matters stood, Article 42 of the Charter should be applied since there was not time for the application of Article 41. The operation of Article 42, however, was thwarted by the fact that no such "special agreements" existed as provided for in Article 43. The Soviet delegate was not present at the Security Council, and had he been, he would no doubt have exercised the veto. In other words, it was a sheer impossibility to apply Article 42. In this predicament, the Security Council decided to make recommendations—which it actually did on 25 and 27 June—concerning measures to be taken for the restoration of international peace and security on the basis of Article 39 of the Charter. Based upon its acknowledged right of recommendation, the Security Council passed the resolution that members of the United Nations should lend assistance to the government of South Korea, and abstain from assisting North Korea. Some fifty-two states indicated their support for this resolution and, in conformity with the main objective of the resolution, seventeen states in different ways made positive contributions to the United Nations military action.

The military actions taken in Korea by various members of the United Nations were firmly founded on the Charter, being in conformity with such recommendations as were provided for in Article 39. Were Mr. Hayashi's point of view accepted, the United Nations would be incapable of taking measures against any patent aggression or violation of international peace and security because the veto could paralyze the functions of the Security Council. This confused position arose from an assumption that military actions by the United Nations are not justified if they are not based upon Article 42. All members of the United Nations are obligated to take such measures as are prescribed in Article 42, while it is left to the free judgment of states whether or not to accept recommendations based upon Article 39. Hence, there is, from the legal point of view, a wide difference between measures taken under Article 42 and recommendations made under Article 39. However, insofar as states accept recommendations based upon Article 39, the effect may be similar to that produced by a decision taken in accordance with Article 42.

With these rather technical discussions as a background, "a resolution concerning the operation of the Peace Treaty" was laid before the House of Councillors on 28 April and passed the same day:

> Whereas the Peace Treaty has come into force this very day and this country, as an independent Power, has now returned to the community of nations; and
>
> Whereas this result is most gratifying to the Japanese people and for this we extend our profound thanks to the friendly Powers;
>
> Be it, therefore, resolved by the House of Councillors
>
> (1) That Japan is determined throughout to contribute to maintenance of world peace and furtherance of the welfare of mankind, and desires admission to the United Nations at earliest possible date;
>
> (2) That Japan will strive to establish good-neighbour relations with the Asiatic countries, so that she may contribute to attainment of world peace;
>
> (3) That Japan will further the solution of territorial matters on a just basis and strive for the establishment of equal opportunity and reciprocity in international economic relations, so that her economic self-support may be assured; and
>
> (4) That Japan will adhere throughout to democracy, emphasize the national morality, develop the spirit of independence and self-defence, so that she may become in name and substance a useful and responsible member in the community of nations.[13]

## PRESS DISCUSSION: THE PEACE TREATY WITH JAPAN AND THE SECURITY TREATY

The trend of thought expressed in organs of public opinion concerning the Peace Treaty and the security problem paralleled the main line of discussions in the Diet.

[13] *Proceedings in the House of Councillors*, 13th Sess., No. 34, 28 April 1952, pp. 5-6.

In 1951, when the time was getting ripe for concluding a peace treaty, the interest of the Japanese people was sharply focussed on the nature of the treaty and the question of Japan's security following its conclusion. Those who held to the ideal of peace with all countries were never quite reconciled to the draft treaty. But it was clear to everyone that, under the existing circumstances, in which the United Nations forces and the Communists were in heated conflict on the Korean peninsula, it was impossible to conclude peace with both sides on equal terms. To insist upon an all-inclusive peace despite this situation would only have resulted in retarding the conclusion of a peace with the majority of the members of the United Nations through the good offices of the United States. Thus the main current of public opinion inevitably turned toward support for this alternative.

The problem of Japan's security after the end of the occupation remained. Everyone acknowledged that theoretically it was appropriate for the United Nations to guarantee Japan's security, but there were doubts about the actual effectiveness of the United Nations and the alacrity with which it could act. The inevitable conclusion was the practical solution of having Japan's security guaranteed by a treaty with a particular nation and with the backing of the United Nations.

*Yomiuri* on 29 January 1951 expressed doubts as to the extent to which Japan could depend on the United Nations security system. "We believe that, in case the peace treaty does not include the Soviet Union as a signatory, the most desirable means for providing for Japan's security would be through a treaty with the United States." This represented the consensus of practical opinion on this matter, and it was felt that since this type of security arrangement is based on the right of "individual or collective self-defense" mentioned in Article 51 of the United Nations Charter, it would be a link with, and would not be in contradiction to, the United Nations security system.[14]

[14] See also *Yomiuri*, 14 Feb. 1951.

On the other hand, a very logical and understandable warning was issued by *Asahi* on 9 February 1951: "Since the continued presence of foreign armed forces in Japan after the conclusion of a peace treaty would have very delicate bearings upon national sentiment, intelligent measures must be taken to guard against antagonisms." But the general trend was to favor the Peace Treaty and the Security Treaty as conceived by the United States special envoy, John Foster Dulles, and adopted at San Francisco.

When the Peace Treaty went into force on 28 April 1952 it brought an end to the military occupation of Japan. The occupation army of the Allied Powers was replaced by the garrison forces of the United States under the terms of the Japanese-American Security Treaty. These were to assume the responsibility for Japan's security.

## ADMISSION TO THE UNITED NATIONS

When a proposal for requesting admission to the United Nations was introduced at the 13th Session of the Diet, it met with strong opposition from a few members. Hyakuro Hayashi of the Communist party stated:

> It is quite a farce that Japan should make overtures for admission to the United Nations before effecting the immediate withdrawal of the U.S. occupation forces from Japan and the complete restoration of Japan's sovereignty from the hands of the U.S. so as to make her an independent state in fact as well as in name.[15]

Likewise, Ikuo Oyama denounced the United Nations for its "interference" in the internal affairs of Korea, its refusal to admit Communist China, and its failure to base its judgment on law. He concluded that Japan's admission should not be sought until the United Nations gained enough common sense to admit Communist

[15] Japan, National Diet, *Official Gazette, Minutes of Proceedings in the House of Representatives*, 13th Sess., 8 May 1952 (author's translation). Hereinafter referred to as *Proceedings in the House of Representatives*.

China and to revoke those actions which appear to be in defiance of the Universal Declaration of Human Rights.[16] In favoring the application, the Left Wing Socialist party emphasized the desirability of "respect for the Constitution of Japan" and "the strengthening of unity in the United Nations." According to their view, the United Nations was a "cripple" as a peace organization because of its biased activities and administration. Japan's participation would be possible only on condition that the United Nations became a more universal organization. The tide of opinion in favor of Japan's participation in the United Nations, however, held sway in the Diet, resulting in approval of the application.

In the press, similar sentiments in favor of Japan's application for membership in the United Nations had been expressed. *Mainichi* observed on 13 March 1952:

> With the implementation of the Peace Treaty just around the corner, the government will shortly take steps to join the United Nations. It will seek approval by the Diet on the pertinent documents. The steps currently being taken are based upon the preamble of the Peace Treaty signed at San Francisco which expressly states Japan's intention of becoming a member of the United Nations. But we approve of the proposed measure not merely because it is mentioned in the preamble of the Peace Treaty (which is, so to speak, a mere legal technicality) but because the aim of the world organization may be summed up as the maintaining of peace and security in the world. The Japanese nation does not lag behind the rest of the world by even an inch in its desire for world peace. Therefore, it is only natural that Japan, which will shortly become independent with the coming into effect of the Peace Treaty, desires to join the United Nations.

After expressing the general hopes of the people of Japan, *Mainichi* referred to the significance of the action taken by the United Nations in Korea:

---

[16] Japan, National Diet, *Official Gazette, Proceedings in the House of Councillors,* 13th Sess., 4 June 1952 (author's translation).

> There are some who say that it is all right for Japan to join the United Nations, but they do not at all want Japan to become a partner in any recourse to force, as in the case of the United Nations action in Korea. But once Japan becomes a member of the United Nations, it is natural that it should have to share responsibilities to some extent.

The example of Sweden, which sent to the Korean front only a medical corps without sharing in the combat, was cited as an illustration of the theory that the duty of sharing in joint action by the United Nations is not unilaterally imposed upon any particular nation.

Of course, in the light of the Soviet veto power, the prospect of Japan's joining the United Nations was not bright. However, *Mainichi* pointed out on 13 March 1952 that in order to strengthen the United Nations, it is natural that every nation that desires to join the Organization should be permitted to do so. At the same time it expressed hope that the desire of Japan would be acceded to, considering the fact that Japan was already a full member of many of the specialized agencies affiliated with the United Nations, such as the International Labour Organisation, the Food and Agriculture Organization, the United Nations Educational, Scientific and Cultural Organization, and the World Health Organization.

After having been approved by the Diet, Japan's application for United Nations membership was formally submitted to the United Nations on 23 June 1952. The Security Council discussed the application on 18 September, and after a heated exchange between the United States delegate Warren Austin and the Soviet delegate Jacob Malik, a vote was taken. The United States and nine members approved and Malik cast the only dissenting vote, as was expected. Thus, because of this negative vote, Japan's application was rejected.[17] However, the General Assembly took up the matter at its seventh

[17] Security Council, Official Records: 7th Yr., 602nd Mtg., 18 Sept. 1952, pp. 1-15.

session and on 21 December 1952 affirmed by a vote of 50 to 5 with 4 abstentions that Japan was qualified to become a member and had the ability and will to carry out its duties.[18]

On 30 January 1953 Foreign Minister Katsuo Okazaki made the following statement in the Diet concerning the General Assembly resolution:

> My belief is that no small political effect was produced by the formal recognition by 50 members of the United Nations that Japan was a peace-loving country and willing and able to perform the duties set forth in the Charter.[19]

The government emphasized that Japan, as "a responsible member of the community of free nations," should act in conjunction with the United Nations and that Japan should continue to look forward to participating in the United Nations as a regular member[20] even though the immediate possibility of membership was very uncertain.

It may be said that the attitude of the Japanese people toward the United Nations and what they considered to be the most serious defect of the United Nations Organization were most symbolically indicated by these two facts: firstly, that Japan applied for membership and that its qualifications for membership were attested to by fifty member nations; secondly, that despite this, the veto exercised by a single nation, the Soviet Union, obstructed Japan's admission.[21]

---

18 General Assembly, Official Records: 7th Sess., 410th Plenary Mtg., 21 Dec. 1952, p. 479; and General Assembly Resolution 620(VII)B, 21 Dec. 1952.

19 *Proceedings in the House of Representatives*, 15th Sess., 30 Jan. 1953 (author's translation).

20 In this connection Foreign Minister Okazaki on 14 Feb. 1953 stated in the Foreign Affairs Committee of the House of Representatives, "While the idea of quasi-membership was once a subject for discussion in the Diet, the government now questions whether it is wise for Japan to join the United Nations on inferior terms as compared with an ordinary member of the Organization. Admission should be applied for in a dignified manner" (author's translation).

21 For further discussion on Japan's quest for admission to the United Nations, see below, Chapter 12.

# EVALUATION OF THE STRUCTURE AND ACTIVITIES OF THE UNITED NATIONS

## PART TWO

*chapter six*

# The General Character of the United Nations

The United Nations, under the provisions of the present Charter, has a dual role: firstly, it is a forum for international discussion and, secondly, it is an instrument for collective security. In the performance of the second of these roles (which appears to be more significant than the first), the United Nations is expected to exercise the functions of mediation and conciliation for the "pacific settlement of disputes" and to take effective measures, including enforcement measures, for dealing with breaches of the peace. The Security Council has the primary responsibility for taking these measures. Every permanent member of the Council, however, has the power of veto and this has been a great obstacle to prompt and effective action by the Council. Nevertheless, although responsibility for the maintenance of international peace and security under the present Charter is conferred primarily on the Security Council, the General Assembly is also authorized to perform certain functions in this field. Therefore, the United Nations, notwithstanding the weakness mentioned above, may still act as an instrument of collective security.

The United Nations has not functioned adequately in respect to the maintenance of international peace; the expected results in this area have not been forthcoming. In practice, the United Nations has acted chiefly as a forum for the international exchange of opinions.

Although a great number of disputes have been submitted to the Security Council and the General Assembly for peaceful settlement, in most cases the two organs have not been successful in bringing about pacific settlements. They have only succeeded in providing a means for an exchange of opinions.

The record of the activities of the United Nations indicates that any dispute to which a major power has been a party or in which it has had important interests has been merely a subject for discussion. In such cases, the United Nations has been unable (except in the Korean conflict) to take decisive measures, such as enforcement action. The disputed matters the United Nations has been able to settle by peaceful means have been, as a rule, cases in which the great powers had no direct interests. Unfortunately, it may be noted, those successful cases have been few.

It must be admitted that present international circumstances make it very difficult for the United Nations to be anything other than a forum for the exchange of opinions. This is, in the last analysis, due to the confrontation of two camps pivoted on the United States and the USSR. When the United Nations was established, it was expected that relations among the major nations would, to some extent, be co-operative and friendly. It was strongly stressed that world peace could only be preserved by the co-operation of the powerful nations and it was also believed that friendly relations among them were essential for the healthy development of the United Nations. But these expectations have not been realized. Opposition between the United States and the Soviet Union has gradually deepened to the point where they have become antagonistic on every issue. It is only natural that the maintenance of peace and security by the United Nations has become very difficult in the absence of co-operation among the powerful nations. Under the circumstances, it could scarcely be expected that the United Nations could function effectively.

In addition to the above-mentioned difficulties, there is a fundamental defect in the Organization itself. Because the major nations have a veto power in the Security Council, they can block any measures by the Council that they think may be disadvantageous to their interests.

By virtue of this power, the powerful nations can vote down action even on trifling cases. The Soviet Union has done so in many cases. It is possible that, even if the veto power had been abolished, the Soviet Union would not have withdrawn from the United Nations or resorted to force to block resolutions of the Security Council on matters of minor importance. However, it is clear that, due to the veto, the United Nations has often been unable to take effective steps even with regard to minor disputes.

The replies to the questionnaires sent out by the Study Group charged with the preparation of this report showed overwhelming support for the view that the United Nations should be not only a forum for the exchange of opinions but also an instrument of collective security. There was, however, some recognition of the fact that it would be difficult for the United Nations to be more than a forum and that it would have to be content with such a role in view of the present world situation.

The opinions expressed in government circles stressed that, according to the Charter, the United Nations is undoubtedly an instrument to maintain peace and this function must be retained and strengthened if possible. In practice, the primary function of the United Nations has been facilitating the exchange of opinions, and this has indirectly contributed to the maintenance of peace and security. Through the discussions in the United Nations, the world can learn the opinions of opposing countries. People then can judge which side is right and world public opinion does not support those who break the peace. Furthermore, in the past disputing nations have often resorted to armed force when they had no opportunity to exchange views and clarify misunderstandings. The more opportunities there are for exchanging opinions, the less chance there is that nations will resort to military action. Therefore, the function of the United Nations as a forum has a special significance.

In the opinion of the members of the Study Group, the United Nations is important as a forum for the exchange of opinions, but the importance of its other functions should not be underestimated. Many members of the Group stressed the point that the United Nations as an organization for maintaining peace should be strengthened despite the difficulties in realizing this aim. It is admitted that the establishment of strong regional organizations for maintaining peace and security outside of the United Nations is unavoidable under the present international circumstances. But it is vital that the United Nations not be weakened or allowed to remain only as a forum for the exchange of opinions.

It is necessary to encourage improvement in the United Nations as a forum for the exchange of opinions for, in the interests of maintaining international peace, the world needs a place where the two camps can talk together. It has been stated that the strengthening of the United Nations is more desirable than the establishment of a new peace organization that excludes the Soviet Union. One of the members of the Study Group, commenting on a conference of one of the United Nations specialized agencies which he had attended, noted that when Soviet representatives did not participate in a meeting, the discussion was monotonous and lacked seriousness of purpose. When they were present, the discussions became lively and the delegations of the free nations became studious and earnest.

Free discussions among nations with differing opinions is an effective means of promoting mutual understanding and agreement.

Contacts between two opposing camps within the Organization will facilitate the understanding of each other's circumstances and points of view. This practice undoubtedly checks the outbreak of war. Furthermore, the people of the world can judge various nations from the reports of the discussions in the United Nations; they can make their reactions known; and they can rebuke those who break the peace. In view of these facts, the function of the United Nations as a forum for the exchange of opinions has special importance and it has made a remarkable contribution to world peace.

However, the United Nations should not remain merely a forum. It must play its role as an instrument in the maintenance of international peace and security. This is, in the last analysis, the original aim of the United Nations, unmistakably stipulated in the Charter. Because of the opposition of two worlds, the co-operation of the leading nations cannot be expected. Furthermore, because of the veto power of the major nations in the Security Council, it must be admitted that it is very difficult for the United Nations to function effectively. But as there have been some cases where the aim of peace has been furthered, we cannot doubt that the United Nations has been a useful institution for maintaining international peace. This is the true character of the United Nations, and the institution should be strengthened in order that it can fulfill this primary purpose.

*chapter seven*

# The Maintenance of Peace and Security

Although the most important purpose of the United Nations is to maintain international peace and security, the veto of the great powers has prevented the Organization from carrying out this purpose effectively. It is, therefore, imperative to discover how this benumbed organization can be reorganized to function in the manner anticipated a decade ago. This is the main subject with which amendments to the present Charter and proposals for the reorganization of the United Nations will be concerned. In this connection, there are three approaches: firstly, to limit the use of the veto; secondly, to transfer some functions from the Security Council to the General Assembly where no member has a veto; and thirdly, to utilize regional security arrangements as a supplement to the universal instrument of collective security.

## LIMITATION OF THE VETO

The underlying cause of the difficulties the United Nations faces can be found in the present situation of the world itself. Unless the conflicts between the United States and its allies and the Soviet bloc can be dissolved or at least eased, it will be impossible for the two groups to co-operate for the maintenance of international peace. Within the United Nations, this worldwide confrontation is apt to be aggravated by the use of the veto power. Limitation on this veto power is therefore one method for strengthening the United Nations.

Regarding "action with respect to threats to the peace, breaches of the peace, and acts of aggression," that is, the matters covered in Chapter VII of the Charter, the veto principle will have to be retained. Its abolition would perhaps be ideal but, in the present situation of international society, the great power veto in this area will have to be accepted.

The maintenance of international peace and security depends primarily upon co-operation among the great powers. Should a breach of the peace, an act of aggression, or an international dispute which might lead to a breach of the peace occur in the present international society, a settlement cannot be accomplished without their co-operation. Should one of the great powers refuse to co-operate, restoration of international peace would become quite difficult. Moreover, should the United Nations venture to take enforcement action against a great power, this might precipitate a third world war and lead to the destruction of the United Nations itself.

When the United Nations was established, it was widely held that the co-operation of the great powers was necessary for the United Nations to maintain international peace and security. At the Dumbarton Oaks Conference, where the original draft of the Charter was discussed, the great powers were unanimously agreed on this point.

Mr. Cordell Hull, who, as the United States Secretary of State, was directly concerned with the Dumbarton Oaks Conference, wrote that:

> There was no question in our minds . . . that the vote of the permanent members of the Council should be unanimous on questions involving security. This was the so-called veto power. We were no less resolute than the Russians in adhering to this principle. . . .[1]

Mr. Edward R. Stettinius, who was Chairman of the United States Delegation at the Dumbarton Oaks Conference and succeeded Mr. Hull as Secretary of State, has also stated that: "There was no question at Dumbarton Oaks as to the necessity of unanimity of the great powers with respect to enforcement action. . . ."[2] Later, in his book *Roosevelt and the Russians,* Mr. Stettinius wrote:

> The sharpest disagreement on voting in the Security Council related to the vote to decide substantive questions. Great Britain, the Soviet Union, China, and the United States had to decide whether or not they would accept as binding all the decisions made by a majority of the Council. A straight majority vote on substantive as well as on procedural matters would mean that the armed forces of any major nation could be used without its consent, quite likely as the result of a vote cast largely by nations which had few armed forces to contribute.
>
> At Dumbarton Oaks, none of the four major powers was willing to accept this situation. They all agreed that the only way each of them could be safeguarded was by adding the requirement that any majority of the Security Council had to include the concurring votes of the permanent members—or, in other words, the right of each major power to veto decisions.

---

[1] Cordell Hull, *Memoirs* (New York: The Macmillan Co., 1948), Vol. II, p. 1638.

[2] U.S. Dept. of State, *Report to the President on the Results of the San Francisco Conference by the Chairman of the United States Delegation, the Secretary of State*, Publication 2349, Conference Series 71 (Washington: Govt. Printing Office, 1945), p. 71.

> The military and naval staffs working with the State Department . . . had insisted on the right of the United States to veto decisions involving the use of American military forces. The armed forces would not recommend to the Senate a world organization that permitted American forces to be used without the express permission of the United States.
>
> Most of the civilian experts in the State Department and advisers, too, agreed on the need of the veto in all matters involving the use of economic sanctions and armed forces. The fact, for instance, that a major argument against American participation in the League of Nations had been that membership would commit us in vital matters was of real significance in determining American support of the veto power by the permanent members.[3]

On the basis of the reports and records quoted above, it may be safely concluded that not only the Soviet Union but also Britain and the United States asserted most positively the necessity of the great power veto in matters relating to the maintenance of peace and security and, especially, to any enforcement action taken to deal with breaches of the peace. It may be assumed that it is impossible to place restrictions on the veto power in this connection and that any attempt to do so will be unanimously rejected by all the major powers.

Regarding the pacific settlement of disputes—that is, the matters covered in Chapter VI of the Charter—the veto should be abolished. It is theoretically justifiable and practically possible to abolish the veto power in matters of pacific settlement. Indeed some nations, among them major powers, have declared themselves ready to agree to such a change.

As provided in Article 27, paragraph 3, a party to a dispute, even if it is a major power, is prohibited from participating in the voting on decisions concerning the settlement of that dispute.

---

[3] Edward R. Stettinius, *Roosevelt and the Russians: The Yalta Conference* (New York: Doubleday and Co., 1949), pp. 18-19.

Heated discussion has repeatedly taken place among the major powers concerning this provision of the Charter. For instance, despite colossal efforts, the major powers did not reach agreement on this point at Dumbarton Oaks. At this Conference, the United States and Britain argued that the parties to any dispute should abstain from any voting on decisions relating to that dispute. They asserted that for a party to vote in such a case would infringe the most fundamental maxim of modern jurisprudence: "No one should be judge in his own cause." However, the Soviet Union obstinately opposed this position and the Dumbarton Oaks Conference finally closed with this problem unresolved.

On 5 December 1944 the late President Franklin D. Roosevelt presented a proposal on this problem directly to the late Soviet Premier Joseph Stalin. Two months later, at the Yalta Conference, the Russians, in what amounted to a major concession, accepted the United States proposal, which became the basis of Article 27 of the Charter.

Although a great power cannot use its veto in a dispute to which it is a party, it can block a decision by the Security Council on other disputes, even those involving a nation with which the great power is in intimate relationship. This has frequently occurred in the Security Council ever since its establishment. The veto was designed to protect the vital interests of great powers, but it is unreasonable to argue that it is necessary for a great power to have the right of veto in disputes to which it is not a party. Since a great power cannot exercise its veto when it is a party to a dispute, it is logical to abolish the veto in cases where the great powers are not parties to the dispute.

Furthermore, the Security Council is only empowered to make *recommendations* for the pacific settlement of disputes; parties are under no obligation to accept them. If a state considers that a recommendation is disadvantageous, it need not follow it. Thus, it can be said that, since a recommendation is not compulsory, there is no reason why a great power should have a veto.

At the San Francisco Conference the major powers, in explaining their opposition to the move to restrict the veto in matters of pacific settlement, put forward the "chain of events" theory. The joint statement made by the Sponsoring Powers at the Conference reads in part as follows:

> No individual member of the Council can alone prevent consideration and discussion by the Council of a dispute or situation brought to its attention. . . .
>
> Beyond this point, decisions and actions by the Security Council may well have major consequences and may even initiate a chain of events which might, in the end, require the Council under its responsibilities to invoke measures of enforcement. . . . This chain of events begins when the Council decides to make an investigation, or determines that the time has come to call upon states to settle their differences or make recommendations to the parties. It is to such decisions and actions that unanimity of the permanent members applies, with the important proviso . . . for abstention from voting by parties to a dispute.
>
> To illustrate: in ordering an investigation, the Council has to consider whether the investigation—which may involve calling for reports, hearing witnesses, dispatching a commission of inquiry, or other means—might not further aggravate the situation. After investigation, the Council must determine whether the continuance of the situation or dispute would be likely to endanger international peace and security. If it so determines, the Council would be under obligation to take further steps. Similarly, the decision to make recommendations, even when all parties request it to do so, or to call upon parties to a dispute to fulfill their obligations under the Charter, might be the first step on a course of action from which the Security Council could withdraw only at the risk of failing to discharge its responsibilities.[4]

---

[4] *Documents of the United Nations Conference on International Organization, San Francisco, 1945* (New York: United Nations Information Organizations, 1945), Vol. XI, p. 712.

According to the above theory, if the Security Council proceeds beyond the consideration and discussion of a dispute, the procedure may well lead to enforcement action and, because of the significance of such action, it must be subject to the unanimity of the great powers. But there seem to be some fallacies in this theory. A recommendation by the Council concerning the pacific settlement of a dispute does not necessarily lead to enforcement action because a recommendation is not compulsory. In accordance with the present Charter, enforcement measures are strictly limited to situations falling within the scope of Chapter VII. They cannot be taken in connection with the pacific settlement of disputes but only when there is a threat to the peace, breach of the peace, or act of aggression. Consequently, it is impossible to justify the veto by relying upon the chain of events theory.

This conclusion is supported by the interpretation Prime Minister Churchill seems to have given to the Charter. Mr. Stettinius graphically described the details of the Yalta Conference when the Prime Minister concurred with the American proposal on voting procedure in the Security Council.

> He [Churchill] had looked at the whole matter from the point of view of British interests . . . and he did not think the American proposal would harm British interests. For instance . . . if China should raise the question of the return of Hong Kong, both China and Britain would be precluded from voting with regard to the method of settling the controversy, but in the last analysis Great Britain would be protected against any decision adverse to her interests through the exercise of the veto right under paragraph III (Removal of threats to the peace and suppression of breaches of the peace) of the Secretary of State's analysis. . . .
>
> Under paragraph III, Great Britain would have the right by its veto to stop all action against Great Britain by the Security Council. Great Britain thus would not be required to return Hong Kong unless she herself agreed to do so. China would and should, however, have the right to speak, and the same

> would apply to Egypt in regard to the Suez Canal. The same considerations, he felt, would apply in the event, for instance, that Argentina made a complaint against the United States.[5]

Although the major powers when parties to a dispute have no veto, they are protected against unfavorable decisions because of the fact that the decisions relating to pacific settlement, being no more than recommendations, have no binding force. As for the Suez Canal or Hong Kong, Great Britain is under no obligation to accept the recommendations of the Security Council, whatever their content may be. Should any threat to or breach of the peace be caused by the hostile acts of Egypt or China and should the Council then wish to take measures, Great Britain could reject them through the exercise of its veto. The conclusion is that recommendations for the pacific settlement of disputes differ absolutely from decisions for enforcement measures and, therefore, to justify the necessity of the veto under the plea of the chain of events theory is quite absurd.

Furthermore, it can be clearly seen from Article 10 of the Charter that the General Assembly has as much power as the Security Council in relation to the pacific settlement of disputes. Recommendations of the General Assembly cannot be blocked by a great power veto. This is proof that the veto in pacific settlement of disputes is not a necessity. If the General Assembly is able to work without the veto, then why is it impossible for the Security Council to do without it?

Since the establishment of the United Nations, some of the major powers have seemed ready to accept the abrogation of the veto power in regard to pacific settlement of disputes. In June 1948 the United States Senate approved a proposal by the late Senator Arthur H. Vandenberg, who was then the chairman of the Senate Committee on Foreign Relations, that the United States support an amendment to the Charter for the abrogation of the veto in

---

[5] *Roosevelt and the Russians, op. cit.*, pp. 145-46.

connection with the pacific settlement of disputes and the admission of new members to the United Nations.[6] The Committee on Foreign Affairs of the House of Representatives also approved a recommendation that the United States strive to limit the use of the veto through voluntary action by the great powers.[7] On 18 January 1954 Secretary of State John Foster Dulles declared at a meeting of a sub-committee of the Senate Foreign Relations Committee that it might be necessary to reconsider limitation of the veto within the scope of Vandenberg's plan, that is, in the field of pacific settlement of disputes and the admission of members.[8] Since one of the most powerful states in the world, namely the United States, is actually upholding the limitation of the veto, it is not an impracticable and utopian idea.

For the reasons stated above, it may be concluded that the veto should be abolished with respect to pacific settlement of disputes. The abrogation of this power will certainly strengthen the United Nations in maintaining international peace and security. This conclusion accurately corresponds with the prevailing opinions of the experts and scholars in Japan and was the consensus of opinion within the Study Group.

## STRENGTHENING THE GENERAL ASSEMBLY

In order that the United Nations may function effectively for the maintenance of peace, the veto should first be limited. As this is a very difficult task, it is desirable that the maintenance of peace and security be made effective through the General Assembly. In other words, the General Assembly should be able to act in place of the Security Council when the Council, because of the exercise of the veto, fails to perform its functions.

---

[6] U.S. Dept. of State *Bulletin*, Vol. XIX, No. 472 (18 July 1948), pp. 79-80.

[7] U.S. House of Representatives, 80th Cong., 2nd Sess., *Report of the Ctte. on Foreign Affairs on H.R. 6802: United Nations Participation Act* (Washington: Govt. Printing Office, 1948), p. 42.

[8] U.S. Dept. of State *Bulletin*, Vol. XXX, No. 762 (1 Feb. 1954), pp. 171-72.

As a means of strengthening the General Assembly, it may be appropriate to utilize the provisions of the "Uniting for Peace" resolution. This resolution was adopted by the General Assembly in 1950 after it became difficult to take action on the Korean issue because of the hostile activities of the Soviet representative in the Security Council.

The pertinent part of the resolution reads as follows:

> If the Security Council, because of lack of unanimity of the permanent members, fails to exercise its primary responsibility for the maintenance of international peace and security in any case where there appears to be a threat to the peace, breach of the peace, or act of aggression, the General Assembly shall consider the matter immediately with a view to making appropriate recommendations to Members for collective measures, including in the case of a breach of the peace or act of aggression the use of armed force when necessary, to maintain or restore international peace and security.[9]

The resolution also provided for the calling of an "emergency special session" of the General Assembly on the vote of any seven members of the Security Council or by a majority of members of the United Nations.

Various measures were taken in accordance with this resolution during the Korean War. For example, on 1 February 1951 the General Assembly called upon the People's Republic of China "to cause its forces and nationals in Korea to cease hostilities against the United Nations forces and to withdraw from Korea."[10] On 18 May 1951 the Assembly recommended "an embargo on the shipment to areas under the control of the Central People's Republic of China and of the North Korean authorities of arms, ammunition, and implements of war . . ."[11] These measures taken by the General Assembly in lieu of the Security Council made a great contribution

---

[9] General Assembly Resolution 377(V), 3 Nov. 1950.

[10] General Assembly Resolution 498(V).

[11] General Assembly Resolution 500(V).

to the maintenance of peace and security. Use of this experience should be encouraged.

Under the League of Nations Covenant, the Assembly and the Council were both authorized to deal with matters concerning the maintenance of peace. It was intended that the Council would be mainly concerned with such matters. This was clear from the organization of the Council itself. It was composed of a small number of states, including great powers, and was designed to take effective action promptly when an emergency required. Article 4, paragraph 4, of the League Covenant stipulated that the Council could deal "with any matter within the sphere of action of the League or affecting the peace of the world." Article 3, paragraph 3, of the Covenant, contained an identical provision concerning the authority of the Assembly. In other words, the Assembly and Council had exactly the same function with respect to the maintenance of peace. It might not seem logical that the functions of the two important organs of the League of Nations should have been exactly the same. But this was unavoidable because, on the one hand, the great majority of the members of the League were small countries and they had the greater voice in the Assembly; on the other hand, the larger countries occupied a more important position and had a greater voice in the Council. By bestowing equal power upon the Assembly and the Council, the position of bigger as well as smaller countries was protected. The League of Nations thus could better attain its aims of preserving peace.

Contrary to the above, the functions of the General Assembly and the Security Council in the United Nations are different. The primary responsibility for the maintenance of peace and security is conferred upon the Security Council. This system is logical in that it may not be considered appropriate for two organs to have the same function. As they differ in composition, it is natural that they should differ in function. It may be more appropriate to impose the function of maintaining peace on the Security Council, which consists of a small number of states, including all of the major powers. Moreover, since the General Assembly consists of many nations, it may take a long time to convoke it or for the members to agree on a decision. The Assembly, therefore, may not be a suitable instrument for maintaining peace. For these reasons, the duty of maintaining peace is imposed mainly on the Security Council and secondarily on the Assembly.

In view of past experiences, however, it is clear that the Security Council, because of the veto, has seldom been able to take effective measures to preserve peace. This failure of the United Nations must be avoided. Theoretically, the United Nations system is an advance over the League system but, from a practical point of view, the latter was better fitted for maintaining peace. It is therefore advisable to insure that the General Assembly of the United Nations, like the League Assembly, can take proper measures for the purpose of preserving peace. It is impossible to imagine any undesirable consequences. This does not necessarily mean that the Assembly will be put in exactly the same position as the Security Council. The Security Council should retain its primary responsibility for dealing with questions of peace and security, but when the Council cannot fulfill its purpose, the General Assembly should be permitted to take the necessary action.

Even if the General Assembly is to deal with the maintenance of peace, it must be stipulated that it shall act only in case the Security Council cannot carry out its duty. Such a condition did not exist in the League of Nations, where the Assembly and the Council were on an equal footing. But the Charter of the United Nations stipulates that the Security Council shall have the primary responsibility for maintaining peace and this is desirable. The Council should deal with a case first and the General Assembly should handle it thereafter only if the Council cannot exercise its functions because of the veto. In this way, the present fundamental principle of the Charter will be upheld and the General Assembly will not interfere with the activities of the Security Council. The activities of the General Assembly are supplementary to those of the Council and there should be no friction between the two organs.

The idea of strengthening the General Assembly is supported in government circles in Japan and by public opinion at large. Opinions have been exchanged in detail among the members of the Study Group and the consensus favored the strengthening of the General Assembly in line with the "Uniting for Peace" resolution. They were of the opinion that the function of the General Assembly should be limited to making recommendations and that any decision with compulsory or binding force should be avoided. It was also agreed that the General Assembly should act only in case the Security Council cannot exercise its functions.

In their answers to the questionnaires sent out by the Study Group, the intellectuals queried agreed that the General Assembly should be strengthened in accordance with the "Uniting for Peace" resolution; they pointed out that there must be some provision to deal with non-performance of functions by the Security Council; they also stressed that the action of the General Assembly should be limited to recommendations without binding force.

Opinions in government circles are as follows: Until the "Uniting for Peace" resolution was adopted in 1950, it was difficult for the General Assembly to take prompt or effective measures even when the Security Council, because of the veto, was unable to exercise its functions for the maintenance of peace and security. But under the provisions of this resolution the Assembly was empowered to take necessary steps immediately if the Council failed to discharge its duty. This means that the fear that the United Nations could not take any measures for the preservation of peace has vanished. This recommendation was very desirable in the interests of preserving world peace and was, therefore, undoubtedly a great contribution to the successful functioning of the United Nations system.

If a case is transferred to the General Assembly because of a veto in the Security Council, the position of the nation that used the veto will be very unfavorable since resolutions can be adopted in the General Assembly by a two-thirds majority vote. This is unavoidable in view of the general interests of the United Nations. However, the General Assembly should be limited to the adoption of recommendations. It is possible these recommendations may be adopted against the will of the major nation which has cast a veto in the Council. If the Assembly could take binding decisions, the major nation would be in a very disadvantageous position. Such an arrangement cannot be considered proper, as it is contrary to the basic spirit of the United Nations and is too extreme in view of the present world situation. If the decisions of the Assembly have the character of recommendations only, the major nation is less likely to object strongly to the transfer of the case from the Council to the Assembly and even if it did object, the objections would not be justifiable.

As to the measures the General Assembly might recommend, these should include not only provisional measures but also enforcement measures. With respect to the latter, there are arguments that they should be confined to non-military measures but these alone are not effective for maintaining the peace. This point is obvious if we look at the Korean War. The League of Nations adopted non-military measures in the war between Italy and Ethiopia but failed to restore peace. Non-military measures are effective only when the parties involved act in good faith and the case is not serious. The General Assembly, therefore, should have the right to recommend military measures as the last resort. As the General Assembly recommendations will not be binding, the members of the United Nations are legally free to accept or reject the recommendations. Thus, despite the importance of the military measures, the responsibility of the General Assembly is comparatively slight.

It is very important to clarify and specify the powers of the General Assembly for the maintenance of peace by amending the Charter along the lines of the "Uniting for Peace" resolution. There is some argument that the resolution is a violation of the

Charter but this cannot be justified, although the resolution may not perfectly fit the spirit of the Charter.

The "Uniting for Peace" resolution provides that an emergency special session of the General Assembly can be convoked within 24 hours to consider a possible threat to the peace, breach of the peace, or act of aggression, at the request of any seven members of the Security Council or by the majority of the members of the United Nations. The Council itself has never decided whether a decision to convoke the General Assembly is a matter of procedure or not. However, even were the Council to decide that this was a non-procedural decision, the Assembly could also be convoked at the request of the majority of the members of the United Nations. And while this may take some time, it does not violate the Charter.

Article 12 of the Charter precludes the General Assembly from making recommendations on any dispute or situation with which the Security Council is dealing. However, in cases where the Council cannot perform its functions, it may strike the question from its agenda, thus making it possible for the General Assembly to take up the case. The veto does not apply to this decision; it is considered a matter of procedure.

On the basis of the above it can be claimed that the "Uniting for Peace" resolution does not violate the Charter. It is, however, the basic spirit of the Charter that any action necessary for the maintenance of peace and security be taken by the Security Council. The General Assembly can discuss the general principles of the maintenance of peace and security and can also make recommendations on actual issues, but, it is argued, matters requiring action are for the Security Council alone to deal with. In view of this fundamental principle, a recommendation by the General Assembly with regard to enforcement action is believed by some to be contrary to the Charter.

There is a question whether or not a recommendation by the General Assembly for the use of the armed forces violates Article 11, paragraph 2, of the Charter, which stipulates that any question on which action is necessary shall be referred to the Security Council by the General Assembly either before or after discussion. But this provision presupposes that the Security Council is functioning normally. It does not prohibit the Assembly from making recommendations in accordance with Article 10 in case the Council cannot perform its function.[12]

In order to avoid ambiguity, it is desirable that the provisions of the "Uniting for Peace" resolution be incorporated in the Charter. This is particularly necessary since this resolution adds important powers to the General Assembly. It would be very difficult, however, to amend the Charter in this way. Since it would mean an abridgment of the veto, it would encounter objection on the part of those nations which give special importance to the veto. Besides, a long period of time might be required before the amendment would come into effect. Consequently, the resolution should be regarded as effective until the amendment of the Charter is accomplished and in the meantime the General Assembly should be required to act in accordance with the resolution. The resolution itself may not conform to the basic spirit of the Charter but is not contrary to it or in violation of it.

## REGIONAL ARRANGEMENTS

A third method to compensate for the defect in the United Nations security system is through regional security arrangements. At the time the United Nations Charter was formulated, it was recognized that because of the veto in the Security Council, there was a danger that the Council might not be able to take the necessary steps for the maintenance of peace and security. For this reason the provisions concerning regional security arrangements and collective self-defense were included in the Charter.

---

[12] Article 10 was not included in the Dumbarton Oaks draft but was inserted in the Charter at the San Francisco Conference.

The United Nations Charter stipulates that no enforcement action can be taken under regional arrangements or by regional agencies without the permission of the Security Council. Since the veto can be applied on the decision to grant such permission, measures cannot be taken under regional arrangements if one of the great powers is opposed.

To remedy this dilemma, the right of collective self-defense was recognized in Article 51 of the United Nations Charter. The so-called right of collective self-defense means that, if a nation becomes the object of military attack, other nations directly or indirectly threatened by the attack can take joint measures for defense.

In this way, the nations which have interests in common with the nation attacked may jointly oppose the attack, and security is thus guaranteed through the co-operation of these nations. With the recognition of the right of collective self-defense, regional arrangements become powerful security instruments. In general, the regional arrangements or agencies cannot take enforcement action without the permission of the Security Council. However, under the right of collective self-defense, many nations can, on the basis of their own judgment, act jointly without such permission. They will not be hampered by the veto and can take action, including military and other measures.

Originally, it was assumed that the Security Council would take necessary enforcement action, or that the action would be taken by regional arrangements or agencies with the permission of the Council. Since the Council cannot easily perform these functions because of the veto, the right of collective self-defense and regional arrangements are recognized as an indispensable means of security. So long as there is the right of veto in the Security Council, regional arrangements based on the right of collective self-defense are inevitable; they are, so to speak, a necessary evil.

Under the circumstances outlined above, and based on the provisions of the United Nations Charter recognizing the right of collective self-defense and regional arrangements, a number of agreements have been concluded. One of the first examples of such an arrangement was the Inter-American Treaty of Reciprocal Assistance, signed in Rio de Janeiro in September 1947 by all the states in the Western hemisphere (except Canada). By this treaty,

> the High Contracting Parties agree that an armed attack by any State against an American State shall be considered as an attack against all the American States and, consequently, each of the said Contracting Parties undertakes to assist in meeting the attack in the exercise of the inherent right of individual or collective self-defense recognized by Article 51 of the Charter of the United Nations.[13]

A second arrangement is the Treaty of Economic, Social and Cultural Collaboration and Collective Self-Defence, signed in Brussels in March 1948 by the United Kingdom, France, Belgium, the Netherlands, and Luxembourg. Article IV of the treaty states,

> if any of the High Contracting Parties should be the object of an armed attack in Europe, the other High Contracting Parties will, in accordance with the provisions of Article 51 of the Charter of the United Nations, afford the Party so attacked all the military and other aid and assistance in their power.[14]

The third example is the North Atlantic Treaty concluded in April 1949. This is the most important regional arrangement and, needless to say, is directed against the USSR. It was concluded among the countries along the coasts of the North Atlantic, centering around the signatories to the Brussels Treaty, the United States, and Canada, with several other Western European countries also included. At present, there are fifteen members.[15] Article 5 of the treaty states:

> The Parties agree that an armed attack against one or more of them in Europe or North America shall be considered

[13] Article 3, paragraph 1. For text of the treaty, see United Nations Treaty Series, 1948, Vol. 21, p. 95.

[14] *Ibid.*, Vol. 19, p. 57.

[15] The members of NATO are Belgium, Canada, Denmark, Federal Republic of Germany, France, Greece, Iceland, Italy, Luxembourg, Netherlands, Norway, Portugal, Turkey, United Kingdom, and United States.

> an attack against them all; and consequently they agree that, if such an armed attack occurs, each of them, in exercise of the right of individual or collective self-defense recognized by Article 51 of the Charter of the United Nations, will assist the Party or Parties so attacked by taking forthwith, individually and in concert with the other Parties, such action as it deems necessary, including the use of armed force, to restore and maintain the security of the North Atlantic area.[16]

A fourth example is the Warsaw Pact which was concluded on 14 May 1955. In accordance with its provisions, Albania, Bulgaria, Czechoslovakia, Germany, Hungary, Poland, Romania, and the USSR have agreed that

> in the event of armed attack in Europe on one or more of the Parties by any state or group of states, each of the Parties to the Treaty . . . shall immediately, either individually or in agreement with the other Parties to the Treaty, come to the assistance of the state or states attacked with all such means as it deems necessary, including armed force.[17]

In addition to this agreement among the Eastern European nations, the USSR and the People's Republic of China signed a Treaty of Friendship, Alliance and Mutual Assistance on 14 February 1950. It contains provisions directed toward preventing "a repetition of aggression" by Japan.[18] The combined effect of these treaties is a far-reaching security arrangement among the Communist nations to aid each other collectively.

Lastly, mention should be made of the Southeast Asia Collective Defense Treaty (SEATO). The parties to this treaty, which was signed 8 September 1954, are Australia, France, Pakistan, Philippines, Thailand, New Zealand, United Kingdom, and United States. According to Article IV of the treaty, each signatory recognizes that

---

[16] United Nations Treaty Series, 1949, Vol. 34, p. 246.

[17] For text, see *The American Journal of International Law*, Vol. 49, No. 4 (Oct. 1955), *Official Documents*, p. 196.

[18] For text, see Raymond Dennett and Robert K. Turner (eds.), *Documents on American Foreign Relations* (Princeton: Published for World Peace Foundation by Princeton University Press, 1951), Vol. XII, 1950, p. 518.

> aggression by means of armed attack in the treaty area [the general area of Southeast Asia and the Southwest Pacific] . . . would endanger its own peace and safety, and agrees that it will in that event act to meet the common danger in accordance with its constitutional processes.[19]

There are other regional arrangements,[20] but the above are the most important. Clearly, these arrangements are in the nature of alliances, that is, as in past treaties of alliance, the contracting parties promise to aid each other against nations that are not parties to the treaty. For instance, NATO is directed against the USSR. It does not openly mention an attack by a third nation or nations, but that it means a possible attack by nations other than the contracting parties is evident in the phrase "an armed attack against one or more of them in Europe or North America shall be considered an attack against them all." In the light of the circumstances under which the treaty was signed, there is no doubt that it refers to an attack by the USSR. Therefore, it has the same characteristics as the old-time alliance treaties. It is the same with the other regional agreements mentioned above. It is clear from past history and present international relations that agreements of this kind give serious provocation and anxiety to third nations and arouse increased international unrest.

A true security agreement is one that is not aimed at a third nation, but guarantees peace and security among the contracting nations. It is a treaty whereby the parties promise not to resort to armed attack or aggression against one another, and if one of them should violate this promise, the other parties agree to co-operate to repress the armed attack or aggression. A treaty of this kind will not provoke a third nation, or give it cause for concern. The Locarno Pact, to which France, Belgium, Germany, the United

---

[19] For text, see Peter V. Curl (ed.), *Documents on American Foreign Relations, 1954* (New York: Published for Council on Foreign Relations by Harper & Bros., 1955), p. 320.

[20] For instance, the Arab League and the Baghdad Pact.

Kingdom, and Italy were parties, was an arrangement of this kind. Germany and France, and Germany and Belgium, agreed not to resort to war against each other. In case of a violation of this promise, all of the other contracting parties were to come to the assistance of the victim of the attack. This kind of treaty can be called a true security treaty, a point which was stressed in a study of collective security carried out by the League of Nations.[21]

The Charter clearly anticipates regional arrangements of this kind, because Article 52 provides for recognition of regional arrangements or agencies on condition that they conform to the purpose and principles of the United Nations. These purposes and principles are primarily concerned with the maintenance of general international peace and security; they are not aimed at any third nation or group of nations. Clearly, the regional arrangements or agencies intended by the Charter must be true regional security agreements. Mutual assistance treaties aiming at a third nation or group of nations are similar to the former alliance pacts and do not conform to the provision of Article 52. Such treaties (including those based on the right of collective self-defense) may guarantee security among the contracting nations, but they will arouse the anxiety of other nations. This is contrary to the purposes and the principles of the Charter and, when regional arrangements of this kind are adopted too extensively, the interests of the United Nations suffer and the purposes of the Organization are violated.

At the same time, it must be recognized that arrangements similar to former alliance pacts are inevitable under the present international situation, especially when the Security Council cannot take effective measures for security because of the veto. A nation must have its security guaranteed by some means; if it cannot depend on the Security Council of the United Nations, it must adopt the next best method, that is, co-operating with friendly

---

[21] Documents of the Preparatory Commission for the Disarmament Conference, Ctte. on Arbitration and Security. C.A.S. 10 (1928.IX.3) and C.165.M.50 (1928.IX.6).

nations for defense. Therefore, as already pointed out, regional arrangements are a necessary evil.

In the replies to the questionnaires sent out by the Study Group, almost everybody recognized that regional arrangements are inevitable in the present international situation. At the same time the opinion was expressed that, ideally, regional arrangements are not desirable. In the meetings of the special Study Group in Tokyo as well as in other areas, the same views were put forward. We may therefore conclude that the general attitude of the public in Japan is that "ideally" regional arrangements are not desirable and should be limited or abolished if possible; however, they are considered to be inevitable due to the international situation.[22]

Although Article 52 of the Charter provides that the regional arrangements or agencies and their activities must be "consistent with the Purposes and Principles of the United Nations," there is no provision for judging whether they really conform and, if not, what can be done. Therefore, there is a possibility that even if they do not conform to the purposes and principles of the United Nations, they might still remain in effect. On this point, one may say the Security Council has the power of control. When enforcement action is taken by regional arrangements or agencies in accordance with Article 53, the permission of the Security Council is necessary; it might therefore be possible to interpret authorization by the Security Council as a judgment that the regional arrangements or agencies themselves are in accordance with the purposes and principles of the United Nations. However, this is not clearly established in practice, so the argument is rather weak.

It is desirable, then, that this point be clarified. Since the Security Council is primarily responsible for the maintenance of peace and security, it would seem appropriate for the Council to examine the matter and decide whether particular regional security arrangements are in accordance with the purposes and principles of the United

[22] For a discussion of Japan's possible participation in a regional security arrangement, see below, pp. 216 ff.

Nations Charter. However, because of the veto right of the great powers, decisions cannot easily be reached by the Council. It would be impossible for the Council to decide that a regional arrangement involving a great power was contrary to the purposes and principles of the United Nations. Therefore, this function should be vested in the General Assembly, where there is no veto right and the opposition of one big power would not interfere with a decision. Decisions on this matter by the General Assembly should require a two-thirds majority vote. Thus, regional arrangements would not be rejected unless they were clearly against the purposes and principles of the United Nations. In any case, it is only natural that the United Nations should exercise control over regional arrangements to ensure that they are in accordance with the purposes and principles of the United Nations.

Although the present Charter stipulates that enforcement action under regional arrangements must be approved by the Security Council, such permission is not easily obtained because of the veto right. If such action cannot be taken, there is danger to the peace in that aggression may be freely undertaken. To avoid this, it is desirable that the General Assembly also be authorized to approve such action. When the Council is carrying out its duty properly, the General Assembly should not, of course, interfere with its business, but when the Council cannot give the necessary approval, the Assembly should be empowered to do so.

The exercise of the right of individual and collective self-defense is, under the present Charter, entrusted to the individual judgment of nations and does not come under the control of the United Nations. The nations are free to decide for themselves whether circumstances require the exercise of this right, and the permission or approval of the Security Council or other organs of the United Nations is not necessary. Past history shows that the right of self-defense has often been abused. Aggressive attacks have often been undertaken in the name of self-defense. Therefore, it is extremely dangerous to let nations exercise the right of self-defense of their own free will. It is necessary that the exercise of this right be properly controlled by an international agency. The same is true with regard to the right of collective self-defense.

The present Charter of the United Nations does not leave nations entirely free in this respect. According to Article 51 of the Charter, measures taken in the exercise of the right of collective self-defense must be reported to the Security Council immediately; and the Charter states that these measures "shall not in any way affect the authority and responsibility of the Security Council" to take necessary action to maintain and restore international peace and security. The Security Council should therefore be able to exert considerable control over the resort to the right of collective defense. However, there is the danger that because of the veto, the Council will be unable to exercise this control. Therefore, in this case, too, it is necessary for the General Assembly to take over when the Council cannot take the necessary action. A decision by the Assembly in this matter should be by a two-thirds majority.

Under present regional security arrangements those nations participating in the arrangement may exercise their right of self-defense collectively, but each individual nation is free to decide what action it will take. A nation must immediately defend itself if it is attacked directly by arms; it must immediately exercise its right of self-defense. It is only natural that a nation should do so, and at least initially take action on the basis of its own judgment. The right to act in this manner was recognized by the International Military Tribunal (Europe) and the International Military Tribunal for the Far East after the end of the Second World War.[23] However, the conditions are a little different for the other members of a regional

[23] The judgment of the International Military Tribunal (Nuremberg) states: "Whether action taken under the claim of self-defense [is] in fact aggressive or defensive must ultimately be subject to investigation and adjudication if international law is ever to be enforced" (*The American Journal of International Law*, Vol. 41, No. 1 (Jan. 1947), p. 207). This implies that the right of self-defense may be initially exercised by a state at its own judgment, although it is finally subject to international adjudication. See also *Judgment of the International Military Tribunal for the Far East* (1948), Chapter 3, p. 31.

arrangement, which are not themselves directly attacked. The action of these nations in coming to the aid of the country which is directly attacked is in the nature of enforcement action. A decision to take such action should not be left to each individual nation but should be taken jointly by all nations participating in the regional arrangement; they should confer and decide whether or not to give aid to the nation attacked. This will prevent a particular nation from taking action, on its own initiative, under the name of the right of collective self-defense. The above decision may be made by a majority or by two-thirds of the nations participating in the regional arrangement. In any case, it would be desirable for the nations participating in a regional arrangement to confer, and exercise the right of collective self-defense by mutual consent.

This point was particularly stressed by some of the members of the Study Group because of the special circumstances of Japan. Japan has in the past engaged in aggressive action in the name of self-defense (the Manchurian Incident and the China Incident, for example). Therefore, experienced people in Japan are extremely wary of the right of self-defense. It would be very dangerous for one nation to invoke the right and take military action on its own initiative. It would be more desirable for the decision to be reached on the basis of the judgment of many nations. Secondly, there is considerable opposition to rearmament in Japan because in the Constitution Japan has renounced war and abolished armaments. Even if Japan's "security forces" are built up and Japan should come to have military strength, there are many who are bitterly opposed to dispatching men for the defense of foreign countries in the name of mutual defense. There are some who are especially anxious over the possibility that troops will be dispatched on the basis of a decision by one country only. If the decision is taken at a conference of many nations, then the opposition against military action for mutual defense will not necessarily be so strong. In this connection, too, it would be desirable that the decision be made by a majority of the nations concerned.

On the basis of the foregoing, the provisions in the Charter regarding the right of collective self-defense should be amended. The underlying concept of Article 51 of the Charter is inappropriate. The idea of self-defense is to take action toward defending a right or interest of one's own which is in imminent danger. This is an established rule of international law. But, under the right of collective self-defense, a nation may act when there is no actual attack or even imminent attack on its rights or interests. Nations which are closely related to the victim of an armed attack are, it is true, anxious lest they be attacked in the future. But for a nation to exercise the right of self-defense and take military action when it has not yet been directly attacked and is in no imminent danger of attack, would be contrary to the idea of self-defense. It is really giving assistance to an attacked nation and taking sanctions against the attacking nation.

Nevertheless, the legal technicality of calling such action the exercise of the right of self-defense provides a pretext for evading the veto. To take enforcement action or sanctions, the permission of the Security Council would be needed, but because of the veto, there is the possibility that permission might not be easily obtained. So in such a case, the right of self-defense is invoked, and without the permission or decision of the Security Council, actions of mutual defense can be taken. As long as the veto right exists, this situation is inevitable. However, we cannot deny the fact that as a result, the concept of the right of self-defense can be unjustly enlarged and the idea of self-defense thus abused.

If the United Nations system for the maintenance of peace and security is altered by strengthening the General Assembly, as we propose, it will be possible for the General Assembly, by a two-thirds majority vote, to authorize enforcement action. Thus, such action will not, as hitherto, be hampered by the veto right. In that case, invoking the right of collective self-defense in order to solve the dilemma brought about by the veto will no longer be necessary. Therefore, Article 51 should be revised so that the provision will cover only the original right of individual self-defense. Joint assistance given by other nations to an attacked nation should be interpreted as an enforcement action for the maintenance or restoration of peace, not as an act of collective self-defense. Such joint assistance can be considered as enforcement action based on the United Nations Charter or, if the provisions regarding regional arrangements are modified, the measures can also be considered as based on regional arrangements.

*chapter eight*

# Membership in the United Nations

As the United Nations was originally established as a *general* international organization, its ideal has been to maintain peace and security throughout the world and to settle economic, social, and cultural problems through the co-operation of all the states in the world. From this point of view, each and every state was expected to become a part of the international machinery of the United Nations.

## CONDITIONS FOR ADMISSION TO THE UNITED NATIONS

As to requirements for admission of new members, the Charter provides that:

> Membership in the United Nations is open to all other peace-loving states which accept the obligations contained in the

> present Charter and, in the judgment of the Organization, are able and willing to carry out these obligations.[1]

If any country really desires to be a member of an organization, it is quite proper that the country be called upon to accept and fulfil the obligations of the organization.

According to the interpretation given by the Allied powers during the Second World War, the Axis powers were not considered "peace-loving states." But now that the tyrannical militarism, which led the people of the Axis powers to the threshold of annihilation, has been eliminated, and the social and political institutions in these nations have been completely reorganized, and the people are making every effort to achieve peace, it is proper that the former Axis powers should be recognized as peace-loving states and allowed to join the United Nations. In this connection it would be desirable to amend the Charter and eliminate Article 107 and the reference to "enemy states" in Article 53.

It is necessary that the conditions of eligibility for membership in the United Nations should not be interpreted too strictly in considering whether a certain state is really able and willing to carry out the obligations contained in the Charter. There is great danger in applying such abstract conditions arbitrarily. The provision must be interpreted and applied so as not to infringe upon the spirit and principle that the United Nations is to be a universal organization and that each and every state is expected to be a member.

In considering whether a certain state meets these conditions, it may be better, instead of requiring evidence of the existence of such will and ability, to consider whether any outstanding facts exist that prove the lack of will and ability to carry out these obligations. If such facts cannot be verified, the applicant for admission should be admitted. The above interpretation would alleviate the problem of admission to the United Nations and

---

[1] Article 4, paragraph 1.

contribute to attaining the ideal of the Organization: universality of membership.

Needless to say, members must be independent states; that is, a state applying for admission must be recognized as independent by a majority of the members. Although the recognition of the state by other states cannot be considered as a condition for admission to the United Nations, it is not proper to admit to membership a state that is not yet recognized as independent by the majority of the members of the United Nations.

During the first decade of the United Nations existence, many states were denied admission to the United Nations. The difficulties of admission are mainly due to the exercise by the Soviet Union of its veto power. In order to remove these difficulties, therefore, the abrogation of the veto power concerning admission is imperative. There would seem to be two ways to accomplish this. The first is to abolish the right of veto in the Security Council so far as the admission of new members is concerned. Under this plan the procedure stipulated in the present Charter concerning admission would still be followed. The Security Council would make the initial decision and then the matter would be referred to the General Assembly. However, the Council's decision would not be subject to the veto but would be made by an affirmative vote of any seven members. The second plan is to transfer the power to admit new members to the General Assembly where the decision would be made by a two-thirds majority of the members present and voting. The second plan is far more radical than the first. It has the advantage of simplifying the procedure of admission while the advantage of the first plan is that it could be carried out without amendment of the present Charter.

A primary reason for proposing a change is that the major powers do not always have a vital interest in this matter. The veto power was originally designed to insure a consensus of the major powers and to insure their co-operation in matters of great importance, such as the maintenance of peace and security. This substantial privilege should be admitted only within the scope of its original purpose. On the other hand, the principle of the equality of states is the most fundamental premise in present international society, so that a privilege that is contrary to this principle should not be approved, unless there are strong reasons for it. The veto power is just such a privilege. Therefore, it is necessary to place rigid restrictions on the exercise of the veto power. It should be exercised only on important matters in which the major powers have vital interests. To put it concretely, the exercise of the veto power should be limited to matters concerning the maintenance of peace and security.

The admission of a particular state to the United Nations will not in fact greatly affect the United Nations. It is true that admission is an important matter for the applicant because members are subject to the rights and obligations contained in the Charter. However, since the admission of a country to the United Nations is unlikely to effect a momentous change in the Organization, it is not likely to harm the interests of major powers. It is unreasonable for the major powers to assert that they have vital interests in connection with the admission of any state to membership in the United Nations.

In the League of Nations the problem of admission to the League was dealt with by the Assembly and was decided by a two-thirds majority. In view of the fact that this matter was never handled by the Council of the League of Nations, there seems to be no precedent for bringing the matter under the Security Council in the United Nations. The United Nations might have adopted the same system as did the League.

In actual fact, most states applying for admission to the League of Nations were permitted to join without difficulty. The applications of a few states were rejected at the first meeting of the Assembly of the League, but there were convincing reasons why they were not permitted to join. San Marino, Monaco, and Liechtenstein were not admitted because they were very small both in territory and population and could not, in all senses, claim to be truly independent states. They were in the position of protected states. It was accordingly decided that these states lacked the ability to carry out the obligations contained in the Covenant. Not one state that maintained normal diplomatic relations with foreign nations was refused admittance to the League of Nations. Problems of membership were generally decided with unanimity in the League. The case of the Soviet Union was an exception. When the question of Soviet admission was considered by the Assembly in 1934, 39 states voted in favor, 3 states were opposed, and 8 countries abstained from voting.

As mentioned above, admission was decided in the Assembly by a two-thirds majority and this system caused no difficulty at any time. This practice neither compromised the authority of the League of Nations nor interfered with its activities. Therefore, it is highly desirable to amend the procedures of admission to the United Nations; the function of deciding on admission should be transferred to the General Assembly, where the veto power cannot be exercised.

Although there is theoretical justification for the transfer of this function to the General Assembly, with the present confrontation of two camps, this system may give an advantage to one side and a disadvantage to the other. If the admission of any state to membership in the United Nations is to be decided by the General Assembly by a two-thirds majority vote, it may be difficult for a state allied with the Soviet Union to win that many votes. Free states may be easily admitted, but Communist states may be rejected. In order to avoid this partiality, the decisions on admission must conform to the underlying principles of the United Nations that membership should be open to all the countries in the world.

This does not mean the unconditional admission of a state to the United Nations. As the Organization is charged with maintaining peace and security, and members must participate in the exercise of this function, it is necessary to emphasize the importance of their ability to carry out their obligation in this connection. However, the conditions of membership must be interpreted as liberally as possible and applied so as to ensure the universal character of the United Nations. Accordingly, any state which has diplomatic relations with a majority of states should be deemed qualified for admission to the United Nations, so long as there is no outstanding evidence of lack of will or ability to carry out the obligations contained in the Charter.

## POSITION OF NON-MEMBER STATES

There are two points to be considered concerning the position of a state that is not a member of the United Nations. One concerns its participation in United Nations discussions; the other bears on the issue of quasi-membership.

*Participation in United Nations Discussions:* Article 32 of the Charter of the United Nations provides that the Security Council shall invite any non-member state to participate, without vote, in the discussion of any dispute to which that state is a party. This provision is appropriate because a settlement of the dispute without such participation would be impossible. That the non-member state should in such circumstances be denied the right to vote is only logical, for Article 27(3) of the Charter requires even a member of the Council to abstain from voting on decisions concerning the settlement of a dispute to which it is a party. If this is the case for a member, so much more should it be so for a state that is not a member of the United Nations.

According to Article 34, the Security Council may investigate not only a dispute, but also a situation that might lead to international friction or give rise to a dispute. There is no provision, however, for the participation of a non-member state in the discussion of a situation, even if it has a vital interest therein. This is hardly a proper state of affairs from the point of view of either the Security Council or the non-member state especially interested in the situation. It is desirable that such a state be enabled to take part in the Council discussions, albeit without the right to vote. It is true that in the case of a situation, the interested parties cannot always be identified as readily and accurately as in the case of a dispute. This difficulty, however, could be overcome if the Security Council would assume the necessary responsibility.

There is no express provision in the Charter authorizing the General Assembly to invite a non-member state that is a party to a dispute to participate in the Assembly's discussion of that dispute. While such participation is specified in Article 32 in the case of the Security Council, there is no corresponding stipulation for the General Assembly. There is every reason to interpret the lack of any such stipulation in the Charter as an inadvertent omission, for, if such a party can be invited to take part in the Security Council's discussion, there can be no special grounds for its exclusion from discussions in the General Assembly. It is necessary to correct this deficiency and to insert a provision for the participation of a non-member state—without vote, of course—in the General Assembly's discussion of any dispute in which that state is an interested party.

One important fact worth noting in this connection is that whereas the General Assembly can extend such an invitation if it desires, the absence of an express provision on this point is apt to multiply the possibilities that the invitation will not be extended. Herein lies the necessity for a definite stipulation concerning such an invitation. Nor should it be forgotten that Article 32 imposes upon the Security Council an *obligation* to invite a party to a dispute to take part in the discussion of that dispute, even if the party is not a member of the United Nations. Why, then, should not the same duty be imposed on the General Assembly? The fact that the Assembly may extend such an invitation does not in the least detract from the advisability of definitely requiring the Assembly to do so. Furthermore, a non-member should be invited to participate in the Assembly's discussions not only in the case of a dispute but also in connection with situations likely to lead to international friction or to give rise to a dispute. On this point, the above arguments concerning participation in the discussions of the Security Council are equally applicable to the General Assembly.

*The Issue of "Quasi-Membership":* The term quasi-membership is used here to mean countries entitled to participate without vote in discussions in the organs and committees of the United Nations. When the question of Japan's joining the United Nations was brought up for consideration in 1952, a suggestion was made in some quarters favoring recognition of the status of a quasi-member state. Opinion in Japan was divided on this issue with the views of those favoring quasi-membership outweighed by the arguments against the proposition.

Those favoring recognition of quasi-membership based their position on the following grounds: In the first place, for the United Nations to attain its purposes of maintaining international peace and security and promoting international co-operation, participation by the greatest possible number of states is highly desirable. However, the so-called veto stands in the way of accomplishing this end. To overcome this difficulty, it is advisable to recognize quasi-member states so as to facilitate their co-operation in the attainment of United Nations objectives.

In the second place, as already noted, Article 32 of the Charter provides for the participation of a non-member state in certain Security Council discussions. Instead of being confined to the discussions of a particular dispute, the application of this provision might be extended so as to facilitate non-member state participation in achieving the general purposes of the United Nations. There is certainly sufficient room for extension; the enlarged application of the principle underlying the provision in question would justify participation by non-member states in general United Nations discussions and their recognition as quasi-members.

The third argument was based on the presumption that quasi-membership would prove to be a preliminary to formal membership. Participation as a quasi-member in various discussions in the United Nations would afford such participants a chance to prove themselves able and willing to act in conformity with the Organization's purposes and principles. This, in combination with the intimate understanding they would gain through their association with member states, would pave the way for their becoming full members of the Organization. Furthermore, it ought to be considered desirable for any non-member state to participate as a quasi-member in the general work of the United Nations and thus to promote its position in the international community.

Those advocating recognition of quasi-membership were of the opinion that it ought to be accorded by a two-thirds majority of the members present and voting in the General Assembly. It was further suggested by the supporters of quasi-membership that non-member states so recognized should be allowed to take part in discussions in the General Assembly and its various committees but should not possess the right to vote.

One of the principal grounds for opposition to the proposed system of quasi-membership was the unclear status of a quasi-member. For instance, would a quasi-member be called upon to assume any of the obligations specified in the United Nations Charter? Not to assume any obligations at all would be as inappropriate as assumption of all the duties of membership. The question that suggested itself then was which obligations were to be assumed. A second objection to the proposition was that a quasi-member would be granted the right to participate in discussions, but denied the right to vote. This would be tantamount to making light of the position of the quasi-members and would fail to do justice to the opinions of the states participating as quasi-members. Furthermore, as a result, due importance would not be attached to settlement of the membership issue itself. There were a few people who opposed the suggestion for recognition of quasi-membership by means of a two-thirds majority vote. With the world divided into two opposing camps, quasi-membership would inevitably be accorded only to those states on good terms with the majority.

For the reasons enumerated above, Japan's intellectuals were divided on the proposed recognition of quasi-membership, with the preponderant weight, however, on the side of those opposed. A similar attitude was found to exist among specialists in international law and politics and by the generally informed public to whom the Study Group sent its questionnaire. In official quarters the proposed quasi-membership system was also apparently considered inappropriate. In the autumn of 1952, when the membership issue was discussed in the General Assembly, thereby giving prominence to the question of quasi-membership, government authorities seemed at first to take a stand in favor of the proposition. But subsequently this position was changed and in 1953 Foreign Minister Katsuo Okazaki remarked in the Diet that any attempt to seek qualified membership in the United Nations would be less than honorable and would have its drawbacks. He felt that Japan ought to follow fair and above-board methods for attaining formal membership.[2]

## EXPULSION

For the United Nations to expel a member from the Organization can hardly be considered appropriate, and it is desirable that Article 6 providing for expulsion be deleted from the Charter.

To inflict punishment by expelling a member of the United Nations "which has persistently violated the Principles contained in the . . . Charter" would merely mean that the Organization was abandoning its efforts to prevent further violations. This would not contribute to a practical settlement of the difficulty. The United Nations might be better advised to keep such a member within

[2] Japan, National Diet, Foreign Affairs Ctte. of the House of Representatives, 15th Sess., 14 Feb. 1953.

the Organization in order to rectify any breach of agreements by exercising surveillance over the member. This would retain the chance for further consultation and better understanding. It is true that expulsion would deprive the member of the rights specified in the Charter, but it would also release that state from the duties imposed by the Charter. The sanction ought, therefore, to be administered so as to suspend the enjoyment of rights but maintain the status of obligations.

Another reason for eliminating Article 6 is that expulsion runs counter to the fundamental proposition that the United Nations should be a universal organization in which membership should be shared by any and every state. It ought to represent the international community. To enfold all states as members of that community into one well-organized international society is the ultimate aim of the United Nations. There ought to be no member of international society that is not a member of the United Nations, just as there can be no individuals in a state who are not subject to its jurisdiction. Even individuals who have violated the laws of their state should not be expelled from the country but should be retained within and so punished as to lead them toward due observance of the laws. It should be the same with the United Nations.

The third reason is based upon Article 5, which specifies the conditions under which a member may be suspended from the exercise of the rights and privileges of membership. This provision *per se* speaks eloquently against the very idea of expulsion. The application of this article to any undesirable member would be a far more effective sanction than expulsion. In the League of Nations, expulsion was, in the absence of any clause providing for suspension, the only form of sanction against members that violated the principles of the League. The United Nations, however, would be well advised to utilize the sanctions in Article 5 and suspend the rights and privileges of such violators without releasing them from their duties.

The last but not least important argument against expulsion is based upon the lessons of the League of Nations. The clause in the Covenant concerning expulsion was invoked in only one instance, namely, soon after the outbreak of the Second World War when the USSR attacked Finland and was expelled from the League. By expelling the USSR, however, the League could gain nothing by way of preventing Soviet violations but lost much in the reduction of its own universality. The fact may be admitted, of course, that even if the Soviet Union had remained in the League of Nations, it would have been impossible to obtain observance of the League Covenant. In other words, whether the Soviets had been expelled or not, the result would have been the same. However, in perspective, the expulsion appears to have been inadvisable. The reason is plain enough. Once the USSR was expelled, the basis for calling the country to task for its action was definitely shattered, while the chances of negotiating with the Soviets inside the organization were infinitely minimized.

One of the arguments in favor of maintaining provisions for expulsion is that, since applicants for membership in the United Nations are required to meet certain conditions, it is only natural to expel any member that fails to maintain those conditions. It is also argued that, since expulsion is subject to the veto, it can be invoked only against minor states and therefore the United Nations could take such action without great risk of endangering international peace and security. Furthermore, the United Nations need not be afraid that by resorting to expulsion wherever circumstances require, international co-operation will be adversely affected since it is safe to assume that co-operation from the state concerned would be of little account. In short, the advocates of expulsion hold that expulsion of lesser states could not in any serious measure hinder the United Nations in attaining its objectives.

While opinion in Japan is divided, taken as a whole the views of those opposed to the expulsion provision are predominant. It may be concluded that the expulsion system hardly merits general support and that the article providing for it ought to be struck from the Charter.

## WITHDRAWAL

The question of withdrawal gave rise to serious discussions at the San Francisco Conference. Some of the delegates opposed any recognition of a right to withdraw from the United Nations. The reasons were that to permit withdrawal would run counter to the principle of universality of the Organization; that withdrawal might be used as an instrument or threat for forcing undue concessions from the Organization; and that to recognize withdrawal would be tantamount to releasing the withdrawer from the duties specified in the Charter.

Other delegates favored a withdrawal provision on the ground that, since any state is at liberty to seek membership in the United Nations, it ought to be equally free to terminate such membership. Moreover, if membership in the Organization were made permanent, some states might find it difficult to ratify the Charter. At least members should be permitted to withdraw if they are unable to consent to any amendments to the Charter. The following explanatory statement was eventually approved at the San Francisco Conference:

> The highest duty of . . . Members is to continue their cooperation within the Organization for the preservation of international peace and security. If, however, a Member because of exceptional circumstances feels constrained to withdraw, and leave the burden of maintaining international peace and security on the other Members, it is not the purpose of the Organization to compel that Member to continue its cooperation in the Organization.
>
> It is obvious, particularly, that withdrawals or some other forms of dissolution of the Organization would become inevitable if, deceiving the hopes of humanity, the Organization was revealed to be unable to maintain peace or could do so only at the expense of law and justice.
>
> Nor would a Member be bound to remain in the Organization if its rights and obligations as such were changed by

> Charter amendment in which it has not concurred and which it finds itself unable to accept. . . .[3]

By this statement, member states are enabled to assume a virtually unrestricted position in regard to withdrawal.

Such a policy on withdrawal is, however, regarded by some as inappropriate. In their opinion, the universal character of the cause of the United Nations requires that withdrawal not be permitted. The purposes and principles defined in the Charter may be regarded as the fundamental purposes and principles of the international community itself. There can be no member of the international community that does not hold them in due esteem. The United Nations ought at least to assume a position against legal recognition of withdrawal.

Conceivably a member state might refuse to attend the meetings of the United Nations or to co-operate with the Organization on any matters. Such an act would in effect amount to withdrawal. But it should not be treated as *de jure* withdrawal, thus releasing the state from its obligations toward the United Nations, but as a *de facto* withdrawal, whereby the state itself is in default. Whether any sanctions should be applied to such states should be determined in accordance with the circumstances. If, for instance, the state was not violating the purposes or principles of the United Nations, but only rejecting co-operation with the Organization, there would be no need to take sanctions. Appropriate action should, however, be taken to prevent possible violation of the principles of the United Nations. In any case, such a withdrawal should not be legally recognized but the state should be treated as a defaulter, still held responsible for fulfilling its obligations as specified in the Charter.

By no means less predominant in Japan is the opinion that recognition of the right of withdrawal is inevitable. The arguments

---

[3] *Documents of the United Nations Conference on International Organization, San Francisco, 1945* (New York: United Nations Information Organizations, 1945), Vol. VII, pp. 328-29.

in support of this view are similar to those set forth at the San Francisco Conference. It is pointed out that the United Nations is an organization founded on the free will of states, and that there should be no restraint by force on those desiring to withdraw. There is some concern, however, over the breadth of the statement approved at the San Francisco Conference. The statement implicitly recognizes the right of a member to withdraw not only if it finds amendments to the Charter unacceptable, but also if the United Nations proves incapable of maintaining peace, or capable of doing so only at the sacrifice of law and justice. This opens the door for subjective judgment by the prospective withdrawers and raises the dangerous possibility that the right of withdrawal may be abused. On the strength of this conviction, many have advocated placing definite limitations on the conditions under which the right of withdrawal should be recognized. It has been proposed that a state be permitted to withdraw only if it cannot accept a specific amendment to the Charter or if an amendment it favors fails to secure ratification by the required majority.

There remains another problem for further consideration: whether the right of withdrawal ought to be specifically recognized in the Charter. An express provision would, of course, be preferable on the ground of clarity, but if the right of withdrawal is explicitly recognized in the Charter, it may maximize the chances of withdrawal with undesirable consequences incompatible with the universal character of the Organization. In the view of a large majority in the Study Group, it would seem most appropriate for the United Nations to give only tacit recognition to the right of withdrawal.

*chapter nine*

# The Domestic Jurisdiction Principle

Under the Covenant of the League of Nations, international disputes arising from domestic matters were placed outside the purview of the Organization. Article 15, paragraph 8, of the Covenant stated that the Council of the League was to make no recommendation as to the settlement of a dispute arising out of a matter within the domestic jurisdiction of one of the parties. The same principle was made applicable to the Assembly by Article 15, paragraph 9, of the Covenant. It should be pointed out that the domestic jurisdiction clause specifically applied only to the competence of the League of Nations in the field of pacific settlement of disputes; the other activities of the League were not subject to this same limitation.

Under the United Nations Charter, domestic matters are outside the general competence of the United Nations. Article 2, paragraph 7, of the Charter reads:

> Nothing contained in the present Charter shall authorize the United Nations to intervene in matters which are essentially within the domestic jurisdiction of any state or shall require the Members to submit such matters to settlement under the present Charter . . .

In prescribing that the members of the United Nations are not required to submit disputes involving domestic matters for settlement by the United Nations, this article of the Charter is similar to the provision in the League's Covenant. However, the Charter is radically different from the Covenant insofar as it contains a general prohibition against intervention by the Organization in domestic matters. In the Covenant domestic matters were an exception only in regard to the settlement of disputes.

There was, of course, some doubt whether the League of Nations did have the authority in any circumstances to intervene in domestic matters. The League Covenant stressed that the decision whether a matter came within the domestic jurisdiction of a state was to be decided on the basis of international law and it is a principle of international law that no nation may intervene in the domestic matters of another. It must be considered that this principle applies even to an international organization such as the League of Nations. Therefore, even if the League was not, in general, prohibited from dealing with domestic matters, it must be assumed that it could do so only insofar as its action did not constitute "intervention." Similarly, while the Charter stipulates that the United Nations has no authority to "intervene" in domestic matters, there is no rule against its taking up domestic matters so long as it does not "intervene." Within this limitation, the United Nations may take up a domestic issue without violating the Charter. On this basis, it may be said that the difference between the League of Nations and the United Nations is not substantial. However, the fact that the League Covenant did not clearly exclude domestic matters from the general authority of the League, while the United Nations Charter explicitly makes such matters an exception to the power of the Organization, implies some difference for the actual handling of cases.

The above-mentioned difference between the Covenant and the Charter goes counter to the evolution of the international community. Over the years, the relationships among nations have grown closer and their mutual dependency has become increasingly great. Thus, the domestic matters of a nation tend to be of increasing international concern and to call for international treatment. Furthermore, both the number of international organizations created to deal with these problems and the powers of these organizations have been constantly increasing. In this perspective, it is inevitable that the competence of international agencies should be expanded as much as possible. That the United Nations should have less power concerning domestic matters than the League of Nations had is, therefore, contrary to the trend of evolution of the international community. It is an anachronism.

For the reasons mentioned above, it is suggested that the provision in the United Nations Charter concerning domestic matters should be so revised as to take the form of the corresponding provision in the League of Nations Covenant; that is, except with regard to the settlement of disputes, the United Nations should have competence to deal with domestic matters.

Domestic matters have been defined as those which, according to international law, are within the domestic jurisdiction of a state. The League of Nations Covenant used the phrase "a matter which by international law is solely within the domestic jurisdiction of a state." The United Nations Charter makes no reference to international law and refers to "matters which are essentially within the domestic jurisdiction of any state."

In the Dumbarton Oaks proposals for the United Nations, the provision concerning the domestic jurisdiction principle was the same as the article in the League Covenant, but it was revised at the San Francisco Conference and the reference to international law was deleted. The reason for this revision, according to the report by the United States delegation, was that "the body of international law on this subject is indefinite and inadequate. To the extent that the matter is dealt with by international practice and by text writers, the conceptions are antiquated and not of a character which ought to be frozen into the new Organization."[1] However, whether or not a certain matter falls within the domestic jurisdiction of a state has to be determined eventually by international law, that is, by international usage and treaties, since there is no other standard on which the determination can be made. It is, therefore, proper to add to Article 2(7) of the Charter the phrase "by international law" and if the concept of law is at present obsolete as a basis for determining "domestic jurisdiction," it should be given a new interpretation suitable for the new international organization.

While the Covenant of the League referred to matters "*solely*" within domestic jurisdiction, the United Nations Charter reads "*essentially*" within domestic jurisdiction. The reason for this change was explained in the United States report, as follows:

> In view of the fact that, under modern conditions what one nation does domestically almost always has at least some external repercussions . . . it seemed appropriate to look to what was the essence, the heart of the matter rather than to be compelled to determine that a certain matter was solely domestic in character.[2]

The difference between "solely" and "essentially" is, after all, a difference in nuance but "essentially" is susceptible of broader interpretation than "solely." This broader interpretation of domestic matters in turn limits the scope of the authority of the United Nations. This runs counter to the general direction of progress

---

[1] U.S. Dept. of State, *Report to the President on the Results of the San Francisco Conference by the Chairman of the United States Delegation, the Secretary of State*, Publication 2349, Conference Series 71 (Washington: Govt. Printing Office, 1945), pp. 44-45.

[2] *Ibid.*, p. 45.

of the international community. Therefore, "solely" is better than "essentially," but even this term is inadequate in some respects. Thus, it is most desirable to use neither term and to state simply that the United Nations should not interfere in matters which "by international law" are within the domestic jurisdiction of a state.

According to the League Covenant, it was for the League Council itself to decide whether a matter was "domestic." But the United Nations Charter lacks specific provision on this point. The members of the committee on legal problems at the San Francisco Conference concluded that "it is inevitable that each organ will interpret such parts of the Charter as are applicable to its particular functions." It was understood by the committee discussing domestic jurisdiction that this general rule would apply to Article 2, paragraph 7.[3] Thus, if a dispute is being handled by the Security Council or the General Assembly and the question arises whether the dispute concerns a domestic matter, the organ concerned has the right to decide the question. Similarly, if a certain problem is being handled by the Economic and Social Council, it is for that Council to decide whether or not its action might constitute intervention in a domestic matter.

A majority of states at the San Francisco Conference considered that disputes on this question should be referred to the International Court of Justice, but the proposal to this effect did not obtain the required two-thirds vote and it was therefore not approved.[4] The ground for the opposition to this proposal was that the various organs of the United Nations were in principle supposed to be equal and it was not deemed proper to give the Court an authority resembling judicial review. This view has considerable merit in that under the existing Charter domestic matters are an exception

---

[3] *Documents of the United Nations Conference on International Organization, San Francisco, 1945* (New York: United Nations Information Organizations, 1945), Vol. XIII, p. 709.

[4] *Ibid.*, Vol. VI, pp. 509-10.

to the overall authority of the United Nations. However, the ultimate decision should properly be made by the Court, particularly if, as previously suggested, domestic matters are made an exception only to the competence of the United Nations to settle disputes.

Although the initial decisions may be made by the organ charged with the particular question in accordance with the understanding at the San Francisco Conference, the ultimate right of decision should rest with the International Court of Justice.

*chapter ten*

# International Co-operation: Economic and Social

Present-day efforts to secure peace through international organizations, centering around the United Nations, can be roughly divided into two categories. Firstly, there are the efforts to eliminate threats to existing peace, to arrest aggression and other actions which might breach the peace, and to prevent the outbreak of large-scale wars. In the second category are those measures which are not directly concerned with eliminating the imminent dangers of war, but are directed toward the establishment of a basis for world peace by ameliorating conditions that might produce wars.

In addition to the direct and immediate task of maintaining peace, long-range programs to deal with economic and social problems have been instituted by the United Nations. One of the striking features of international organization today, particularly as compared with the past, is that an effort is being made not only to guarantee international security by political and military measures, but also to construct the basis for peace by solving economic and social problems.

## GOALS OF INTERNATIONAL CO-OPERATION

As stated in Article 55 of the Charter, the United Nations is concerned with international co-operation in the following three areas:

(1) higher standards of living, full employment, and conditions of economic and social progress and development;

(2) solutions of international economic, social, health, and related problems, and international cultural and educational co-operation; and

(3) universal respect for, and observance of, human rights and fundamental freedoms for all without distinction as to race, sex, language, or religion.

The achievement of these three goals is not merely the professed mission of the United Nations itself, but also of all its members since they have pledged themselves to take concerted or independent action, in co-operation with the United Nations, to achieve these objectives.

The aims of the United Nations in the last of the fields mentioned above were clarified and made more definite by the Universal Declaration of Human Rights, adopted on 10 December 1948.[1] The Declaration is an international agreement based upon a high moral code. It does not possess a legally binding character, but it is not far from the truth to say that it was indeed an epoch-making incident in the history of mankind when the nations of the world agreed to promote respect for human rights.

In accord with human ideals and the universal demand for social justice, all people, without distinction as to nationality, race, or

---

[1] See General Assembly Resolution 217(III).

color of skin, should be treated equally. On the basis of their rights and dignity as human beings, they should be employed under proper conditions with remuneration for their labors, and should be enabled to live, together with their families, lives worthy of their status as human beings. The methods for achieving this ideal are, on the one hand, through education, science, and culture, and, on the other, through concrete measures developed through international economic exchange and co-operation.

From the standpoint of social justice, it is obvious that there are great disparities among the nations existing on the earth today, differences in the size of territories, in the possession of colonies, in natural resources. To change national borders because of these unequal distributions would mean that one nation would benefit to another's disadvantage. Conflict between nations would be inescapable. Wars occur in most cases when nations, claiming that the existing order is irrational or unjust, try to change the order by actual force. That is the reason why international law esteems the international *status quo* and is very reluctant to change it.

The *status quo* of the international order should be respected. But if an historically determined situation is maintained without rational consideration of possible improvement, a nation attempting to break down the *status quo* is strengthened in the belief that the goddess of justice herself will smile. The social energy necessary to build a "new order" may accumulate to the point of explosion. Therefore, if a lasting international order is to be built upon international law and an international peace organization, it should be based not on the maintenance of a fixed *status quo* but rather on an elastic order that permits "peaceful change." Where the political jurisdiction of a nation is concerned, it is almost impossible to change the *status quo* by peaceful means. As a result, a planned world economy may be the only way by which the nations may smoothly co-operate to bring the international society step by step nearer to the goal of social justice pictured in the Universal Declaration of Human Rights. However high the political fences of nations are, the water of economic exchange will filter through, distributing that which is ample and supplementing that which is lacking. If this natural tendency is augmented by planning, and if nations will strive toward economic co-operation along this line, it is not impossible to improve the living conditions of human beings all over the world without changing any political boundaries. It is not too much to say, in this sense, that the rational adjustment of the international economy is the star of hope for world peace.

*ECOSOC:* Among United Nations organs, it is primarily the Economic and Social Council which handles international economic and social problems. It consists of eighteen nations elected by the General Assembly. Each member has one vote and the decisions of the Council are made by a majority of the members present and voting.[2] Compared with the Security Council, where the permanent members have the veto, or the General Assembly, which can take an important decision only by a two-thirds majority, ECOSOC is the most democratic of the major organs of the United Nations. Furthermore, since ECOSOC is mostly concerned with international economic, social, and technical problems, international conflicts are seldom brought up. The deliberations proceed smoothly as a general rule and in that respect ECOSOC is in striking contrast to the Security Council, which has degenerated into a battleground of power politics. If the nations of the world would save the energy they spend on political opposition and devote it to the planning and execution of constructive work for the international economy, and if they would try to utilize the Economic and Social Council and other organs for that purpose, then it would be possible for these organs to function, as one author says, as seven league boots for the progress of mankind.[3]

However, the very merit of ECOSOC is at the same time its weakness. The Council is an organ for discussion, study, and

[2] Articles 61 and 67 of the Charter.

[3] John MacLaurin, *The United Nations and Power Politics* (New York: Harper & Bros., 1951), p. 307.

recommendation; it has no power to put its recommendations into effect. The Council can prepare draft conventions for submission to the General Assembly on matters falling within its competence, but it is for the sovereign nations to decide whether to adopt, sign, and ratify them. The Council can call an international conference, when necessary, but it cannot determine the conclusions that conference may reach. It can be said that the Council is somewhat detached from the actuality of international politics. Because it is not backed with political power, discussions in ECOSOC are conducted harmoniously, but at the same time, this also means that ECOSOC lacks the power for pressing forward plans of its own making. If ECOSOC were to be reorganized so that it could take decisions on international economic matters with binding force, economic problems would become pressing political problems, and the discussions in ECOSOC would turn into political controversies as in the Security Council.

In developing a planned international economy through the United Nations, the strengthening of ECOSOC becomes a problem. An international committee of the outstanding economists of the world might be established to draw up plans which the Council might discuss and recommend to the General Assembly. The Assembly might in turn be given the authority to take binding decisions in this area. Such a system would be useful for promoting international planned economy in such fields as the development of unexplored resources, the improvement of living standards in underdeveloped areas, and the rationalization of production, distribution, and consumption.

It would be impossible, however, to devise plans that satisfy the national self-interests of all nations. If decisions are to be made by majority vote, and if the policies decided upon are to be put into practice independently by each state, there will be obstacles to the execution of programs and it would be immediately impossible to maintain international harmony. Under such circumstances, it would be better to limit the work of ECOSOC to planning and making proposals without binding force, leaving to the free choice of the nations the decision whether or not to implement the recommendations. The efficacy of the planning would not be so great but if the plans themselves had validity, and if people came to understand that their realization would contribute to international peace and would be in the interests of all nations, the way to a rationally operated international economy might be found. Economic problems concern everyone. Even though a plan seems to be disadvantageous in the short run for some countries, if people understood that, from a broader view, it would benefit the welfare of human beings and the prosperity of all, nations would then choose the path of co-operating toward a planned international economy. The way to solve international economic problems is not by forcible measures of law or politics, but by the rationality of the planning and the strength of truth. Solutions must be built on understanding and agreement.

Therefore, although some may be dissatisfied with the activities of ECOSOC, this organ should not be strengthened in such a way as to give it the power of taking binding decisions. The reason the United Nations is not fully effective in the economic field is that the patterns of thought of the nations and their actual relationships with each other are yet far from the level of the ideals of the Charter. To translate the economic goals of the United Nations into actuality will take a long time. But the basis is to be found in mutual understanding, and this should not be hurried by force. In the technical adjustment of the international economy, it is necessary for ECOSOC to make plans with which the people can objectively agree. For the same reason the delegates to ECOSOC must act as international public servants promoting the welfare of all mankind rather than representing merely their own private, national political interests.

*The Specialized Agencies:* Also important for the long-range construction of world peace are the various specialized agencies connected with the United Nations through ECOSOC. Such organizations as the International Civil Aviation Organization, Universal Postal Union, International Telecommunication Union, and World Meteorological Organization are organs for technical liaison and adjustment in the fields of transportation and communication. They are closely connected with the maintenance of a stable international economy. From the standpoint of the development of the world's economy, other agencies play a far more important role: the International Monetary Fund and the International Bank, which are the organs of international finance; the International Labour Organisation, which tries to solve labor problems and improve working conditions; the Food and Agriculture Organization, which studies and attempts to improve the food situation of the world. Furthermore, the World Health Organization, with its mission of maintaining health and preventing sickness, contributes to guaranteeing mankind's right of existence. The United Nations Educational, Scientific and Cultural Organization (UNESCO) expedites international understanding and co-operation in the educational, scientific, and cultural fields, and at the same time tries to contribute to improving living standards through the utilization of science.

During the period when Japan was denied admission to the United Nations because of the Soviet veto in the Security Council, Japan joined all the above agencies and, as a full-fledged member, participated in international co-operation toward peace. It is difficult for Japan, with no strong armed forces, to make a positive contribution to the United Nations collective security system. Therefore, Japan is all the more anxious to contribute to the long-range construction of world peace through the specialized agencies of the United Nations.

## PLANNING INTERNATIONAL ECONOMY

The principle of democracy which esteems the freedom and creativeness of all who live in society is as pertinent today as it has been in the past. However, the laissez-faire principle of the nineteenth century—under which economic and social activities were left to individual freedom and creativeness with the belief that by "unseen hands" there would be a natural adjustment resulting in the well-being of all—is not applicable today. The day of free economy without planning is past history, and a new era has begun in which more or less systematized planning of the social economy has become necessary. The principle of economic planning should not be restricted to internal regulation within each country but should be enlarged to a scale of international magnitude. What is needed for the future is the planning of the international economy.

Today, even in countries where the traditions of free economy are widely maintained, there is considerable economic planning, largely in connection with the exercise of administrative power. In the past, when political power was widely dispersed among local areas and only the simplest forms of transportation had been developed, sections of one nation frequently suffered from famine while in other areas the prices of agricultural produce fell because of the rich harvest. Today, with the establishment of centralization, the development of transportation, and the possibility for national industries to be adjusted according to plan, such irrationalities can be avoided insofar as the domestic economy is concerned. However, in the world as a whole there are conspicuous imbalances of production and consumption, of supply and demand, causing trouble and unhappiness to individuals and to society. While on the one hand there are those living agreeable and convenient lives, enjoying the fruits of modern science, there are also those living in misery far from the dignity due to human beings. While there are some agricultural areas where production cannot be increased, however intensive the methods undertaken, there also exist wide areas, covered with jungles, with natural resources still unexplored. In the world at large, direct communication between raw material areas and industrial areas is more frequently hindered by political barriers than by the natural barriers of mountain range or ocean. Very often the surplus goods of one country take on rare value in distant countries. Planning an international economy, and rectifying the imbalances, is indeed the difference between progress through peace or destruction through conflict.

The basic conditions are different for an economy planned according to domestic politics, and one planned for an international society. Planned economy in a single nation needs to be backed by strong political power to keep the wayward economy on a set track, and to suppress the almighties of centralized capital or monopolistic enterprises. In the international society, however, there is no centralized organization, much less an organization which can even tentatively be considered a world government. Planned economy within one country is difficult enough, but it is infinitely more difficult, if not impossible, to put planning into practice for the international economy. In an international society, all plans are carried out by the will or calculation of the many nations, each insisting on its own sovereignty. It is true that the idea of national sovereignty has lost its former absolute nature in international law, but, without a single centralized authority with the power to issue directives, there is still no way to put into practice economic measures which go counter to the will of individual nations. Therefore, planned international economy at this stage means literally only planning; and there is no organization with the power to push a plan to realization. The planning of the international economy cannot, for example, be accomplished by strengthening the authority of ECOSOC so that its decisions can be forcibly executed.

Under the circumstances, there is of course the danger that efforts will degenerate into paper plans. If the plans of ECOSOC do have an effective influence on the actual international economy, it will be due solely to the fact that the plans themselves are rational and practical. Despite ECOSOC's lack of power, if the solutions it suggests to economic and social problems are rational and applicable to the actual situation of international society, and if the nations find actual advantage or future hope in putting the plans into practice, the plans will not be permanently shelved. In this regard, it is strongly desired that ECOSOC plan boldly to break down the present situation in the international economy, and with persuasive power, based on truth, make proposals to the General Assembly or the affiliated nations.

In the international economy, each nation demonstrates a strong national egoism. The small nations lacking in natural resources, or the underdeveloped countries promoting their own industries, set their tariff barriers high. Even among the rich nations, governments established by the support of the people must, in order to stay in power, follow policies primarily aimed at protecting home industries. So long as this situation continues, however rational are the plans that the United Nations might make about economic relationships in the world, there is little possibility of their being realized. Therefore, the first step toward a planned international economy is to lower the tariff barriers, and move toward free trade. Within one nation, planned economy and free economy are two policies conflicting with each other. However, in the international economy, where each *nation* is one unit, free trade is a premise for planned international economy. The extension of free trade means the breakdown of economic nationalism, and results in the elimination of monopolization of international markets. It plays the role of the New Deal in the international economy. Only on the premise of opened doors of international markets based on free trade would it be possible for nations, in their own enlightened self-interest, to adopt the rational plans proposed by ECOSOC and other related economic organs, and carry them out through agreements with other nations.

Extension of free trade must not mean a return to the unplanned nineteenth century system of free trade, or a return to the international order of the League of Nations period. The free trade system wanted today must be backed by recognition of the necessity for international co-operation for realization of full employment, improvement of real income, increased production, and development of natural resources. It must be based upon the positive will of nations to take measures to realize these aims. Thus the bitter experience of past conflicts of economic nationalism would be fully utilized. It is very necessary to prevent the recurrence of worldwide panic—one of the primary causes of the Second World War—to develop underdeveloped areas and to expedite their industrialization. For the peace of the world, a balance of prosperity in the world must be maintained and peaceful outlets for nationalism must be provided.

Destitution can be the hotbed for destructive ideas. A financial crisis will provide opportunities for Communist expansion. To prevent these developments, the advanced countries must invest in foreign countries and volunteer to decrease tariff barriers. Otherwise, the problem of the dollar shortage in the world cannot be solved, and the unbalanced state of the world economy will become permanent. The United Nations, in expediting the movement toward free trade the world over, must present policies which will establish and maintain an international economic equilibrium. This is not a mere application of the principle of free economy to the international society; it would mean combining economic freedom with economic control, based on international agreement. For instance, along with the efforts to make free trade universal, such measures as supranational control of iron and coal, as undertaken in Western Europe under the Schuman Plan, should be taken up on a worldwide scale.

## IMPLEMENTING THE BRETTON WOODS PLAN

The plan to reorganize postwar international economy along the line of free trade was clearly evident in the Bretton Woods Agreement. The organization of the international exchange economy, supported by the three pillars of the International Monetary Fund, the International Bank, and the proposed International Trade

Organization, was a departure from the nineteenth century idea of an international free economy. Free trade without planning is not a basis for maintaining the equilibrium of world economy, but serves to allow those countries with outstanding economic power to dominate the world market at their will. On the contrary, the Bretton Woods system is based on the principle of international co-operation aiming at balanced economic development, and it must in that respect be highly praised as a marked advance compared with the prewar international economic order.

The United Nations system attempts to promote measures for improving access to raw materials, developing markets, and adjusting the relations of the "Have" and "Have-Not" nations by peaceful means. On the one hand, it was the aim of the International Trade Organization to promote free trade by means that would guarantee the possibility of peaceful changes. Organizations like the Fund and the Bank, on the other hand, are trying to further capital investment under international auspices.

The plan established by the Bretton Woods Agreement is not quite free from the economic nationalism that has hitherto dominated international economic relations. It can be said that it is a less than harmonious mixture of nationalism and internationalism. This defect was revealed in the arguments which preceded the Bretton Woods Agreement and became even more evident when such major nations as the United States and the United Kingdom failed to ratify the Charter of the International Trade Organization. (Thus, it never came into existence.) By adhering to economic nationalism and betraying international co-operation, nations interfere with the operation of international organizations and bring a loss to themselves by denying the fundamental spirit of the United Nations. Therefore, it is desirable that nations, especially the major nations composing the central force of the United Nations, suppress their economic egoism, and, with a view to the long-range construction of world peace, take positive action for the realization of the plans laid down in the Bretton Woods Agreement and the Charter of the

International Trade Organization. These should not be allowed to remain simply ideas.

## THE UNDERDEVELOPED AREAS AND INTERNATIONAL PEACE

It is obvious that the cancer threatening international peace today results from the fact that the economic development of the underdeveloped areas has long been neglected. Their natural resources were utilized for the benefit of the advanced countries while the living standards of the natives remained at a level unworthy of human dignity. As a result of the Second World War, many former colonies gained political independence. Even though they gained political independence and their peoples regained a long forgotten freedom, without an accompanying economic improvement the appearance of many new independent nations in the world may only threaten the stability of world order. The bonfires of nationalism are burning along the southern boundaries of the Eurasian continent, from North Africa through the Near East and South Asia to the Far East. As a result there is stormy conflict in international relations. Behind these struggles there is always some latent economic problem giving justification to those who challenge the historically conditioned order.

These facts lead to the conclusion that expediting the economic development of underdeveloped areas and improving the living standard of these areas are urgent prerequisites for world peace. The United Nations was right in aiming from the very start at the solution of economic and social problems and in putting special stress on the development of underdeveloped areas. From the standpoint of establishing the basic conditions for peace, the chief expectation from the United Nations lies not in its security functions, but in a rational adjustment of the world economy.

It is regrettable that under the circumstances, as long as there is imminent danger of war, the energy of the United Nations will be exhausted on the immediate problem of preventing an outbreak of war, leaving economic problems, which respond only to long-range efforts, to be dealt with later. The major countries of the United Nations know that the old situation of an armed peace still prevails today; they cannot help spending much effort and money toward building up armaments, and thus they cannot afford to devote their major energies to the economic activities of the United Nations. Furthermore, economic nationalism in the advanced countries prevents the United Nations from realizing its high ideals. Hurriedly formed measures to prevent war are often themselves fraught with the danger of provoking wars, whereas long-range plans to deal with the causes of war not only are free from this kind of danger, but each measure is to some extent effective in rectifying the present situation. The United Nations, and the major countries affiliated with it, should reflect deeply on the fact that the wagon of peace can go steadily forward only on the two wheels of security and economic development, not on the wheel of security alone.

The key to the development of underdeveloped areas is the utilization of science and technology and the introduction of capital. Utilizing natural energy through science to serve humanity, and developing unexplored natural resources through the use of technological skills, are the two gospels of modern civilization. The backwardness of the underdeveloped areas results from the fact that they have never been privileged to share in the benefits of these gospels. In the future, the dominant societies must not prosper over other people; measures must be taken so that the welfare of all human beings will improve by the wider application of science and technology. The fact that UNESCO is making it possible for the desert to become green by the irrigation of arid zones, and is trying to fructify barren areas through the study of tropical humid zones, is worthy of record in the history of mankind as ambitious pioneer work in the development of underdeveloped areas. The United Nations technical assistance program tries to improve the living conditions of the underdeveloped areas by modernizing the production systems in these areas. For technical assistance to be effective, the people of the underdeveloped areas must have enough knowledge and experience to utilize the newly introduced methods. It is only through education that progress can be made. Therefore, technical education must precede technical assistance; initial assistance must be given in the form of technical education. In this sense, it is appropriate that the United Nations technical assistance program should be carried out with the co-operation of UNESCO, and that the latter should continue its work in the field of technical education and the exchange of personnel.

The development of underdeveloped areas is, however, too big a problem to be solved merely by technical assistance. Underdeveloped areas lack their own capital, and no industry, even with the aid of science and skills, can rise without capital backing. As the report of a group of the specialists appointed by ECOSOC has stated:

> It is only through the rapid growth of the capital equipment of the underdeveloped countries that the vast problem of disguised unemployment in agriculture can be overcome; and it is only through the rapid growth of production and real income of the underdeveloped areas that the world economy as a whole can attain that steady rate of growth that would permit the needed structural adjustments to be brought about without a contraction of world trade.[4]

As Mr. Hokom Tshand of Afghanistan has said: "Any programme of technical assistance, however well prepared it might be, would be of no use if it were not followed closely, if not accompanied, by capital investment."[5]

Investment in underdeveloped areas must be in accord with the interest of the areas themselves. The development of these areas

[4] United Nations Doc. E/1584, *National and International Measures for Full Employment*, Dec. 1949.

[5] General Assembly, Official Records: 4th Sess., 2nd Ctte., 90th Mtg., 3 Oct. 1949, p. 20.

cannot succeed unless based upon the ideals of the United Nations. These are basically different from the principles normally governing the export of capital which usually involve the exploitation of colonies. Capital, of course, because of its very nature, will not flow toward areas where there is no interest to be gained or where it will be obviously impossible to expect a return on investments. It will be possible to prevent indiscriminate or unwise investments only through adequate planning with assured prospects of return on the capital invested. Short-term profits should not be the determining factor in the export of capital to the underdeveloped areas; long-range investment must be facilitated. Priority must be given to the kind of investment which will assist the underdeveloped areas to develop their own industries, thus relieving unemployment and helping to improve living conditions. Unless precautions are taken in this regard, Article 55 of the United Nations Charter and Article 23 of the Universal Declaration of Human Rights[6] will degenerate into mere phrases. The first problem to be solved in the rational reorganization of the world economy is the implementation of a long-range investment program, adjusted and planned by the United Nations and its agencies.

In this connection, the Bretton Woods system, and especially the International Bank, is very important. To develop industries and promote an expanding world economy, the financial organ should be a wing of the United Nations Organization, and it should be so operated as to serve the nations that, according to objective standards, need capital. Of course, the International Bank at present lacks the resources to meet the wide need for capital in the underdeveloped areas. Its operations have been supplemented by special international arrangements such as the Marshall plan and the Colombo plan. Unilateral foreign investment plans, even if they do not serve as an outlet for disguised economic nationalism,

---

[6] Article 23 of the Declaration provides that all people have the right to just remuneration for work of their own choice, ensuring for themselves and their families an existence worthy of human dignity.

attract suspicion, and may provide food for adverse propaganda. It is, therefore, desirable that international investments for the development of backward areas gradually be brought into a unified system under the aegis of an objective international organ such as the International Bank. The Bank could then operate in accordance with reasonable plans for the international economy; but to accomplish this, the resources of the Bank must be expanded in order that it may meet the acute demands of various areas in need of development.

## REGIONALISM IN INTERNATIONAL ECONOMY

As economic life becomes more complicated, it becomes difficult for a nation to meet the production and consumption needs of its "national economy" through reliance on its own resources. As a result, economic relations among nations become increasingly interdependent. In view of such factors as distance, differences in political and social systems, transportation facilities, level of living standards, etc., there is reason to believe that it is more appropriate to begin, not with the adjustment of worldwide economic relations, but with planning the economy of a more or less integrated area, and then to consider the interrelationships among various areas. The concept of "Grossraumordnung" in international relations, as propounded by Carl Schmitt in the late 1930's,[7] was nothing but a program for the new Nazi order. Still there is a certain logic in dividing the world into geopolitical blocs and in considering separately the economic planning for each such bloc. Actually, the world today is divided into two major blocs: one, the Communist sphere centering around the USSR, and the other, the opposing bloc of free nations. It is possible, and even necessary, to consider the free world as a combination of several smaller units. While Carl Schmitt advocated a closed, regional economic bloc aiming at self-sufficiency, what

[7] See Carl Schmitt, *Völkerrechtliche Großraumordnung mit Interventionsverbot für raumfremde Mächte* (Berlin: Deutscher Rechtsverlag, 1939).

is needed today are "open, regional economic spheres." These should not conflict with the idea of the universality of the United Nations, but should occupy an intermediary position between the economy of the whole world and the economy of each national unit.

Regionalism in the economic sense is in a way analagous to the regional approach to collective security. For instance, it is obvious that Western Europe today consists of one closely-knit bloc, not only politically and militarily, but also in the economic sense. The postwar recovery of this Western European bloc was achieved under the Marshall plan, and it shows promise of increased economic development. In comparison with Western Europe, Asia is so large an area, with such varied civilizations, that it is very difficult for the Asian nations to coordinate their progress. However, the nations of Asia have much in common; they share certain semi-colonial characteristics resulting from their historical background, their industrial backwardness, and low standards of living. In planning an international economy, and particularly in solving the problems of developing the underdeveloped areas, it is not too far from the truth to consider that the nations of Asia have strong mutual bonds. The Economic Commission for Asia and the Far East has already been active in research and in developing the natural resources in the area. For the solution of the economic problems of the whole of Asia, similar activities should be undertaken in the fields of finance and trade.

Asia today possesses a very complicated political structure. From the standpoint of security, the question arises whether a system like NATO might not be necessary for Asia. Such a security system in Asia would naturally be opposed to the Communist sphere and would take on the appearance of preparations against Communist aggression. But in Asia there are "neutralist" nations like India and Burma; moreover, continental China, with its vast area adjacent to the Soviet Union and its great population, is now a major nation in the Communist sphere. (Even those nations in Asia which are associated with the free world are divided economically between the dollar and sterling blocs.) Under the circumstances, Asia cannot be considered a homogeneous political unit. In view of this situation, the economic improvement of Asia as a whole must be based on a mitigation of the opposition between the free world and the Communist sphere, and due regard must be paid to the economic relations between the free Asian countries and Communist China. On the other hand, if the political need to protect Asia from the threats of Communism takes priority over other considerations, some way must be found by which the other Asian countries can become economically independent even if cut off from Communist China. If political measures for the defense of Asia are taken without appropriate steps for the solution of the economic problems of those Asian countries outside the Communist sphere, then the measures of political defense will themselves eventually prove fruitless.

From the standpoint of the regional development of the Asian economy, the position of Japan needs special consideration. The former Japanese ambition to secure most of Asia as a market and a supplier of raw materials for Japan's economic and militaristic needs stirred up an intense nationalistic passion and resulted in aggression against China, and the adventure of the Pacific War. The idea was similar to the ambition of the Nazis who tried to create a European order with Germany as the center and Africa as the raw material area. The scheme for a "Greater East Asian Co-prosperity Sphere," as it was known during Japan's militaristic era, was shattered by defeat. No remnants of this former egocentric co-prosperity idea should be allowed to influence Japan's attitude toward economic regionalism in Asia today. It is true that objectively there are special economic problems common to Asian countries, and that Japan does occupy a unique position in the Asian economy because of its combination of industrial ability and poor natural resources. In the successful planning of a regional economy, much would depend upon whether Japan's peculiar position is utilized or neglected.

Japan is one of the "advanced" countries in Asia. Progress in science and modern technology, however, has not reached the level obtaining in North America or Europe. In present-day Japan, progress and backwardness intermingle; furthermore, the country is overpopulated, and short of arable land and raw materials. It is not a simple question to decide what place Japan should have in the regional economy of Asia. Its skills and industrial abilities, its geographical position, and the general level of living standards in Asiatic countries, seem to justify a primarily industrial role for Japan. If Japan can have access to the raw materials of Asia and turn them into manufactured goods to fill the needs of various areas in Asia, this will not only facilitate Japan's economic independence, but will also improve the living conditions of the Asian peoples.

As already indicated, Japan has joined the various specialized organizations of the United Nations and strongly desires to make a positive contribution to the achievement of United Nations objectives through these agencies. Japan should be able to play a considerable role in the United Nations technical assistance programs. Proper utilization of its special abilities and potentialities will be useful for the development of all of Asia. It is therefore desirable that the United Nations organizations concerned with economic problems and the development of technical skills establish offices in Japan. At the same time, qualified Japanese workers should be employed in the headquarters of these organizations, so that the United Nations in its work for peace can make the maximum use of the abilities of the Japanese people.

## POPULATION

The population problem is a relative problem which concerns the relationship between consumption and production populations. A very large consuming population can be supported, provided it is possible to maintain an equivalent producing population—that is, if the proper relationship of land, raw materials, industrial ability, etc., can be achieved. For instance, it would be possible to feed the present population of an overpopulated country like Japan if the import of raw materials were adequate for the full operation of Japan's potential industrial powers.

When a country cannot support its population, a countermeasure is emigration. Apart from the question whether there is a country willing to receive the immigrants, there are difficulties such as transportation and expenses of emigration. Even if emigration offers only limited possibilities for the solution of the population problem, there is some hope if some possibility for this kind of a solution exists. It can be maintained that providing overpopulated nations with an outlet through emigration would be useful in preventing, at least ideologically, the growth of excessive nationalism. In this connection, it may be noted that the Nazi demand for colonies was put forward as a policy for the solution of the overpopulation problem.

The population problem is primarily a domestic matter resulting from the fact that a nation has not in the past taken appropriate countermeasures, but has simply let the tendency toward increased population take its own course, or even adopted a policy of encouraging an increase in population. The overpopulated nation is itself responsible for its sufferings. Nevertheless, even though overpopulation is brought about by the indiscriminate acts of past generations, it is necessary to consider it from the point of view of the burdens on the present generation. We should seek to understand how the problem developed and take rational measures to repress further increases. Overpopulation is today a cause for unrest in society, and its manifestations in unemployment, low wages, and food shortages pose a threat to basic human rights. If the situation becomes worse, it may well have a disturbing influence on international relations. Moreover, while there are overpopulated nations, there are also vast areas in the world that are sparsely populated and have enormous, still unexplored, natural resources. It would therefore be worthwhile to take up the population problem as one part of a planned international economy. Population could be transferred to underdeveloped areas where it could be productively employed, or natural resources from a raw material area could be made available to overpopulated countries so that they could support their populations. Such measures would help to solve the population problem and improve the welfare of many human beings.

From an international point of view, emigration is the first countermeasure to be considered. It should be planned with the idea of transferring population with the aim of developing the underdeveloped areas. Because of transportation and other difficulties, it cannot be expected that emigration can do much to alleviate the population problem. It is, therefore, necessary to see that the interchange of raw materials and manufactured products between industrial and raw material areas is carried out as smoothly as possible. In planning the national economy of any one country, a major consideration is the development of appropriate links between industrial and raw material areas. This same consideration must be given priority in planning on a worldwide or regional scale, not for the benefit of any one country, but for the benefit of all. To carry out the ideals of Article 23 of the Universal Declaration of Human Rights, plans should be formulated on an international scale to bring about a balance between overpopulated and underdeveloped areas.

The population problem thus has serious international implications, and the United Nations should take more positive action than it has heretofore. At the World Population Conference, sponsored by the United Nations in September 1954, the population problem was taken up from a purely scientific angle. Since it is a very delicate international problem, and even the mere discussion of it may stir up political suspicion and confusion, it is only natural that the United Nations should have approached the problem initially from a purely demographic angle. The handling of the population problem by the United Nations must start with research, and demographic research comes appropriately within the jurisdiction of UNESCO. When the United Nations itself deals with the population problem, however, it should take it up as one aspect of a planned international economy. The United Nations should give advice to the nations concerned as to the appropriate measures to be taken. As the problem is a very acute one not only from the domestic but also from the international point of view, it is necessary for the United Nations to approach the population problem from an objective standpoint based upon careful research.

The United Nations should be especially concerned with emigration as a countermeasure for the population problem. For that purpose, it would be desirable to establish an International Emigration Organization, as a specialized agency of the United Nations, to carry out research on world population. In particular, it should study how immigrants can adapt to the culture and mode of living of the countries to which they immigrate and the attitudes of the nation receiving them. Research of this kind is an important task for the social scientists, and in this regard it would be appropriate to enlist the help of UNESCO. The International Emigration Oiganization should also circulate information to the nations concerned, examine international disputes concerning emigration matters, and investigate the grievances of the countries involved. When necessary, advice should be given to these countries but, since emigration is a domestic matter, it would be impossible for the United Nations to do more than give advice; nor should stronger measures be expected.

## DEVELOPMENT OF MARINE RESOURCES

The sea occupies three-quarters of the world's surface. Everyone knows that the sea is an important supplier of food. Shell mounds found throughout the world are evidence that even in primitive times, man obtained part of his food from the sea. Despite the fact that there has been remarkable progress in the utilization of the sea, the exploration of marine resources is superficial in the light of the limitless possibilities; but today the world stands on the brink of developing the chemicals in the sea and mineral resources at the bottom of the sea. The total quantity of marine resources is enough, and to spare, to meet human needs. As the resources are widely dispersed and diluted, only a small portion is being utilized at present. But in the future, when land resources are exhausted and methods for further exploiting marine resources are developed, the sea will present a new hope for mankind.

The sea is inherently more "international" than the land. Sea water is constantly moved around over extended areas by the currents; men sail to every corner of the sea; and fish and other forms of marine life travel thousands of kilometers. The sea, under the tradition of freedom of the high seas, has no boundaries or customs taxes. Its resources belong to everyone, for all are free to acquire them; but they do not belong to anyone as no one can claim that they belong exclusively to him. John Locke supposed a natural state of human life before governments existed, and said that while natural things belonged to everyone as everyone could utilize them, at the same time they belonged to no one because no one could monopolize them. He tried to clarify the basis of private property from the standpoint of natural law by pointing out that if someone added his labor to the natural things, making them useful for the living of human beings, then they became private possessions.[8] Locke's theory is just a hypothesis as far as the terrestrial world is concerned. But his natural law theory is applicable in principle to the marine world even today. The sea not only possesses inherently international characteristics but has been utilized by all as a natural element; there has hitherto been no positive legislation to regulate the sea.

---

[8] John Locke, *An Essay Concerning the True Original Extent and End of Civil Government* (Second Essay), Chapter V.

Recently, there has been increased recognition of the importance of marine resources, and, as a result, nations are attempting to secure them for their own benefit. Efforts have been made to draw demarcation lines, similar to land boundaries, on the surface and the bottom of the sea, with punishment to be meted out to trespassers. This is not a mere extension of the traditional idea of territorial waters. Boundaries for territorial waters were first established to control smugglers, or arrest criminals, and did not concern marine resources. On the contrary, the new problems arise from the efforts of particular countries to monopolize the known and unknown resources of the sea. Claims to possession of the continental shelf and the practice of designating wide areas in which other nationals are forbidden to fish are attempts to put the marine resources, rich in international characteristics, under national domination. They portend important revisions in the principle of freedom of the high seas.

It is only natural that nations should try to protect their interests in the various types of marine resources. The right to fish in a certain area is often protected by law as an exclusive right for the nationals of one state. Exclusive rights are often claimed with regard to resources that require investment for their development. Recently, veins of coal and oil near the seashore have been explored, and large-scale claims are being staked out on the bottom of the sea. In the light of these developments, it is hardly strange that rights, similar to the territorial rights of a nation, are going to be extended beyond the former narrow territorial waters into the wide ocean.

Even if a monopolistic right over certain areas of the oceans can be recognized, the basis for such rights is a relative one and their range is very vague. If each nation were to insist on a sovereign-like domination over sections of the sea, the ocean, which has long served the welfare of human beings under the principle of freedom of the high seas, would soon become the scene of jurisdictional fights and economic nationalism. The time when nations competed to draw lines on land yet untrodden by human feet and to claim areas as large as their own may recur in the future, this time with regard to the seas. Then it will become inevitable that progress in the development of marine resources will result not in a contribution to the welfare of human beings and the peace of the world, but in new international conflicts which will threaten the peaceful coexistence of nations.

When mineral resources on the continental shelf are the continuation of mineral veins within a particular nation, that nation is partially justified in insisting on its rights in that area. Even if it is impossible to utilize these resources at present, with the improvement of technology, it may be possible to develop the area in the future. On the other hand, if some animals, and especially fish with high mobility, congregate at a certain period in the sea near a particular country, that nation is not justified in claiming that it alone can dominate that part of the sea as a territorial right. A nation does have some right to claim jurisdiction over the waters adjacent to its shores. After all, people's feelings cannot be ignored if they see foreign fishing boats capturing fish in front of their eyes. There are various other new problems, and the possibilities for complicated international conflicts are legion.

If no authoritative international peace organization were in existence, the issues in this field would have to be solved by conflicts and compromises among the nations concerned. With the accumulation of individual compromises, international practice and treaties adjusting the interests of nations would be formulated. Since the United Nations already exists as an organization for adjusting the international economy through rational means, it is desirable that it take the initiative in examining possible incidents, and endeavor to find solutions to any actual international disputes which arise concerning the oceans.

The progress of science and technology is essential in the development of all resources but this is especially true in the case of marine resources. Just as the development of marine resources is a matter of international concern, so the basic scientific study of oceans requires a higher degree of international co-operation. We do not yet fully understand the propagation of marine life which is an important source of food. To carry out research in this field, it is necessary that the nations along the seas enter into joint programs, for steady progress can be assured only through a high degree of international co-operation. Developing this area of research would be a great mission for UNESCO.

The sea is indeed an unknown quantity; but knowledge in this field is gradually increasing. Is any nation free to experiment in the middle of the ocean with a new weapon of unheard-of destructive power? Or, should there be some international regulations against actions that might cause damages or bring unpredictable dangers in the open sea which is to be utilized for the common use of mankind? These problems are a challenge for the United Nations, and this is virgin soil for the development of international law.

# SECURITY, NEUTRALITY, AND ADMISSION TO THE UNITED NATIONS

## PART THREE

*chapter eleven*

# The United Nations and the Problems of the Far East

To evaluate the role of the United Nations with regard to Japan's security it is necessary to consider the general attitude of the United Nations toward the problems that have developed in Far Eastern countries. This leads inevitably to a comparison between the League of Nations and the United Nations in their approach to Far Eastern problems.

A substantial difference between the two international agencies is reflected in their efforts to deal with Far Eastern problems. After the Covenant of the League of Nations went into force on 10 January 1920, many disputes pertaining to international peace occurred in East Asia. But, at least during the first half of the history of the League, they were settled "outside the League of Nations." In contrast, the United Nations has from the outset asserted its jurisdiction in the area and has endeavored to deal with the important problems that have occurred in the Pacific region.

## NATIONAL REVOLUTION IN CHINA

The League's lack of concern with Far Eastern problems was repeatedly demonstrated during the 1920's when the organization stood by idly while grave international disputes arose one after another in China. During this period, China was undergoing severe internal upheavals, and the struggle for power among the different factions and rival Chinese governments led to frequent clashes with vested foreign interests. Although China was a member of the League, none of these numerous incidents was discussed in the League. That it did not intervene in these situations revealed its lack of interest in the Far East and its weakness as an international peace organization.

During the 1920's an intense anti-foreign movement developed in China, and foreign settlements were unilaterally taken over by Chinese authorities. This situation gave rise to the incident of 30 May 1925 (the Shakee-Shameen incident) where marines guarding the British settlement in Canton fired in self-defense upon anti-foreign demonstrators.

On 6 June 1926 the Nationalist government at Canton appointed Chiang Kai-shek Supreme Commander of the Nationalist Revolutionary Forces and sent him north to undertake the conquest of the provincial warlords. In view of the attacks on the British concessions in Hangkow and Kiukiang and in the face of the aggravated situation in the entire Yangtze River region, the British Foreign Minister, Sir Austen Chamberlain, declared in Parliament on 26 January 1927 that Britain was dispatching troops to Shanghai. In an official communication dated 8 February to the Secretary-General of the League of Nations, the British government explained its policy toward the situation then prevailing in China; from the text of the communication it was clear that Britain was merely informing the League of its policy and was not referring the situation to the League for its consideration.

At the time of the northward advance of the Nationalist Revolutionary Army, other powers resorted to various measures for the protection of their interests. In 1927, and again in 1928, Japan sent troops into the Shantung peninsula. In April 1928 both the Peking and Nationalist governments of China protested that Japan's action violated Chinese sovereignty and international law. Yet they did not seek a remedy through the League of Nations.

In May, however, following the Tsinan Incident, the Nationalist government asked the Secretary-General of the League to hold a meeting of the League Council. But at that time the League had not yet recognized the Nationalist government (the Chinese delegate at Geneva was Chu Chao-hsin, a representative of the Peking government). The League did not, therefore, entertain the Nationalists' appeal. The Japanese expedition to Shantung was generally considered excessive for the protection of Japanese interests. If, as China protested, Japan had violated China's territorial integrity, there was ample reason for the League to take up the matter under Article 10 of the Covenant. The reason for the League's inaction may have been that the special conditions in China were taken into account and the League held that the matter was not suitable for consideration by the world organization.

## SINO-SOVIET DISPUTE IN MANCHURIA

Shortly after the Nationalists completed their campaign and the ruler of Manchuria, Chang Hsueh-Liang, was brought, at least nominally, under control, the Nationalist and Manchurian regimes acted in concert to attempt to retrieve Chinese interests in Manchuria—particularly the Chinese Eastern Railway, which had fallen under Soviet control. This led to open conflict with the USSR.

The conflict between China and the Soviet Union was intensified when on 27 May 1929 Chinese authorities raided the Soviet consulate at Harbin and followed this by other provocative acts. In July diplomatic relations between China and the Soviet Union were broken off. In view of the massing of Soviet troops close to the Manchurian border, the Supreme Council of the Chinese government met on 21 July to consider what measures should be taken. The alternatives were: (1) to appeal to the League of Nations, of which China, but not the Soviet Union, was a member; (2) to invoke the Kellogg-Briand Pact, which had been ratified by both disputants and was to come into force within a matter of days; (3) to seek mediation by a third power, such as the United States; or (4) to negotiate directly with the Soviet Union.

The Chinese government decided to try direct negotiations, but preliminary parleys made little progress and negotiations were disrupted after Soviet and Chinese troops clashed at the Manchurian border in August. On 20 August the Chinese government informed the other signatories of the Kellogg-Briand Pact of the situation and declared that it would adhere to the spirit of the pact and was ready to negotiate the dispute with the Soviet Union. In the meantime, Soviet troops had occupied the capital of Tungning Province and shortly thereafter intensified hostilities to an extent which was to force China to a settlement on Soviet terms. China's subsequent appeal to the other signatories of the pact to intervene against the USSR brought only another appeal by them that the disputants should adhere to the pact.

Although any matter which called for invoking the pact should have been automatically a matter of concern to the League, China seems to have thought it best to rely upon the pact rather than to call upon the League. This decision may have been influenced by the fact that the Soviet Union was a signatory to the pact, but was not a member of the League. Even so, an appeal to the League was certainly legally possible. If a dispute arose involving a non-member of the League, the League Council was authorized under Article 17, paragraph 1, of the Covenant to invite the non-member state to accept, for the purposes of the dispute, the obligations of a member. Furthermore, under Article 17, paragraph 3, if the

Soviet Union refused the invitation and later resorted to war against China, the punitive clauses in Article 16 would have been applicable. During the early 1920's there had been several attempts to submit to the League disputes involving the Soviet Union (e.g., the Iranian complaint in 1920 over the Enzeli Affair and the Finnish complaint in 1922 concerning events in Eastern Karelia) but the USSR had refused to co-operate with the League, considering it an instrument of the capitalist nations for preserving their interests.

Thus the Nationalists did not appeal to the League, nor did any other nation urge the League to take action on the issue. The fact that League members such as the United Kingdom, France, and Italy individually called the attention of the two disputants to their duties under the pact[1] shows that the nations did not have much faith in the power of the League of Nations to handle issues of this nature, and that they felt it would be more effective to invoke the new pact.

## THE MANCHURIAN INCIDENT AND THE SINO-JAPANESE CONFLICT

Despite the fact that many important international disputes which occurred in the Far East throughout the 1920's fell within the scope of League activities, they were not referred to the League for settlement. When Japan provoked the Manchurian Incident in 1931, the League finally did intervene. Since this was the first large-scale armed clash since the establishment of the League, it turned out to be a major test of its authority. In retrospect, it may be said that the League's intervention damaged rather than enhanced its prestige. In the final analysis, the League, although nominally a peace organization for the entire world, was in reality an agency primarily to protect European interests. When Japan challenged its authority, the League pressure was insignificant.

[1] This action resulted from the initiative of the United States which was not a member of the League.

That the League of Nations lacked power as a world organization was of course due in part to the fact that the United States and the Soviet Union[2] were not among its members. The Manchurian Incident and the subsequent Sino-Japanese conflict provided these two great powers with an opportunity to approach the League and also to co-operate with each other in pursuit of their common objective, to halt Japan.[3] On 5 October 1931 (soon after the outbreak of the Manchurian Incident) the United States Secretary of State, Henry Stimson, sent word to Sir Eric Drummond, Secretary-General of the League of Nations, that the United States would support, independently, the actions of the League in this matter. He stated that it was most desirable that the League maintain constant vigilance and exercise all its authority in order to control the activities of China and Japan.[4] This was tantamount to a declaration that the United States would maintain a joint front with the League against Japan.

The League, however, proved ineffective in dealing with the Manchurian Incident and the related Shanghai Incident of January 1932. The state of "Manchukuo" was established and recognized by Japan in September 1932 and in March 1933 Japan announced its intention of withdrawing from the League, after the Assembly had recommended a solution along lines unacceptable to Japan.[5]

Nor was the League any more successful in dealing with subsequent hostilities between Japan and China. In September 1937 China appealed to the League, citing Articles 10, 11, and 17 of the

---

[2] The Soviet Union became a member of the League on 18 September 1934.

[3] At this time the United States was the only major power which had not recognized the Soviet Union. In November 1933, however, diplomatic relations were re-established. Thus there seemed to be a greater possibility that the two powers might join forces to counter Japan's expansion on the Asian continent.

[4] U.S. Dept. of State, *Papers Relating to the Foreign Relations of the United States, 1931*, Publication 2476 (Washington: Govt. Printing Office, 1946), Vol. III, pp. 116-17.

[5] In the voting on this resolution on 24 February 1933, Japan cast the only negative vote.

Covenant. It was not until September 1938 that the League responded by invoking Article 17 of the Covenant and inviting Japan to assume the responsibilities of League membership for the purposes of settling this dispute. Japan refused to do so and on 30 September 1938 the League Council declared that, in accordance with Article 17(3), members of the League were entitled to adopt individually the measures provided for in Article 16. Even though the League authorized punitive measures against Japan, their actual effectiveness was inevitably small, since each member state was left free to decide for itself whether or not a situation called for action and, if so, what measures it would take. With this interpretation of Article 16, it was only to be expected that the resolution would accomplish little aside from a moral denunciation by the League of Japan's action.

In brief, from an examination of the record of the handling of these open military clashes between China and Japan, it is apparent that the League lacked global authority to settle international disputes. It can also be said that the League was extremely weak in executing its duties because of the prevailing interpretation that did away with the obligation of members to take concerted action in the application of punitive measures.

## THE UNITED NATIONS AS A WORLD PEACE ORGANIZATION

That the United Nations is, not only in name but in fact, a peace organization of worldwide scope can be seen firstly in the distribution of its membership and secondly in the way it has faced the problems of Asia.

The Far East has been much more fully represented in the United Nations than it ever was in the League of Nations. Japan, China, and Siam were original members of the League, and India, as a member of the British Commonwealth, had separate representation. Iran was also an original member. Of the states which subsequently became members, almost all were European or nations with interests closely related to the European states. Although such states as Turkey, Iraq, Ethiopia, Liberia, Afghanistan, and Egypt joined the League, it continued to be a predominantly "European" organization.

On the other hand, the original members of the United Nations included India, China, and the Philippines. Of the states later admitted to United Nations membership, nine are Oriental nations (Thailand, Pakistan, Burma, Indonesia, Cambodia, Ceylon, Nepal, Laos, and Japan). Of the seven states which on 22 March 1945 formed the Arab League (Egypt, Iraq, Jordan, Lebanon, Saudi Arabia, Syria, and Yemen), five were original members of the United Nations and Yemen and Jordan were later admitted. Libya, another member of the Arab League, has also become a member of the United Nations. The Arab states have shown a firm solidarity within the United Nations and have often taken concerted action with the other states of Asia and Africa. These countries have functioned as a buffer in the cold war and, generally speaking, they may be said to stand for Asiatic interests. Thus it is obvious that the United Nations has far greater Asiatic representation than the League of Nations had and that it is in fact an international peace agency established on a worldwide basis.

Another distinction between the two international organizations is that the League of Nations completely ignored Asiatic matters until 1931 when it took up the Manchurian Incident. Almost all the cases handled by the League up to that time concerned strictly European interests. Of the political issues brought before the League, three concerned Latin American nations; all the rest were primarily matters of European interest. (This included certain Balkan and African problems.) This tendency persisted even after the Manchurian Incident and, aside from handling the later Sino-Japanese conflict as an extension of this Incident, the only other action the League took on an Asian problem was to comply with a request by the Chinese, British, and Indian governments to establish the border between Burma and China.

On the other hand, the United Nations since its inception has grappled with East Asian questions. One of the first political disputes to be considered by the United Nations was the Indonesian question. This and the Kashmir issue, which was later taken up by the United Nations, were both matters related to the independence of Asiatic peoples. After the Chinese Communists won a decisive victory in the civil war, the question which regime represented China became a major issue in the United Nations.

When the war broke out in Korea, the United Nations valiantly intervened and faced an unprecedented trial against the background of the opposition between the East and West. The positive attitude of the United Nations in utilizing all its resources for the solution of Asian problems has been vastly different from the negative approach of the League of Nations under similar circumstances. It may be said then that historical facts testify that the United Nations is truly a *world* peace agency.

## NATIONAL MOVEMENTS AND THE PRINCIPLE OF SELF-DETERMINATION

At the Peace Conference held after the First World War, the principle of self-determination received emphatic approval. At that time, however, application of this principle was restricted to European peoples; the self-determination and independence of non-European peoples were completely ignored. Moreover, even after the establishment of the League of Nations, any movement toward self-determination was considered a matter within the domestic jurisdiction of the nation concerned; the League was not therefore to interfere.

The Second World War stimulated the trend toward national independence among the Asiatic peoples and this movement accelerated in postwar years. Of course, even under the Charter of the United Nations, colonial problems are considered as matters primarily within the domestic jurisdiction of the administering state. Yet if, in the judgment of the Security Council, the disturbance attendant upon an independence movement is considered to endanger or threaten the peace, the United Nations is empowered to intervene. This and the provision concerning self-determination in Article 1(2) establish for the United Nations a basis for handling problems of national independence which is quite different from that of the League. The first concrete case within this category was the issue of Indonesian independence.

The Pacific War was a turning point in the movement of the Indonesian people toward independence. After Japan's surrender it was impossible for the Dutch to re-establish their rule in Indonesia. To cope with this situation, the Allied powers dispatched British and Indian troops to Java under the command of Admiral Lord Louis Mountbatten, head of the Southeast Asia Command. They also requested Japanese forces to maintain peace and order in the region. The Dutch government at this point opened negotiations with leaders of the Indonesian independence movement. This was the situation in Southeast Asia when the Security Council of the United Nations met for the first time in London in January 1946.

Seizing this opportunity, the Ukrainian SSR, inseparably linked to the Soviet Union, requested that the Security Council consider the Indonesian situation. Referring to Articles 34 and 35 of the United Nations Charter, the Ukrainian delegate maintained that the military activities of the British and Japanese armies in Indonesia were aimed against the natives and constituted a threat to international peace and security. He urged the Security Council to conduct the necessary investigations and take measures to end the situation.[6]

The Security Council immediately began discussing the issue. The Ukrainian delegate argued that the intervention of British and Indian armies in Indonesia was in direct violation of Article 1(2) of the United Nations Charter, which deals with the principle of self-determination, and Article 73 on non-self-governing territories.

[6] See Security Council, Official Records (S.C.O.R.): 1st Yr., 1st Series, Supple. No. 1, p. 76.

He proposed that the Security Council set up a commission to "carry out an enquiry on the spot, establish the facts in Indonesia and report to the Security Council on the result of its work."[7] The Egyptian delegate stressed that British troops should not be used against the Indonesian national movement and introduced a proposal expressing the hope that the negotiations in progress between the Dutch government and the Indonesian leaders would result in an amicable accord based on the principles of the United Nations Charter, particularly the right of self-determination.[8]

Neither the Ukrainian nor the Egyptian proposal was approved by the Council. But the fact that so soon after the establishment of the United Nations problems pertaining to the peoples of East Asia were presented to the United Nations for action and were considered by the new world organization, raised expectations that the United Nations would assume heavier responsibilities in this area than the League of Nations had done.

The issue of self-determination and independence for Indonesia went through more complicated developments later. However, at long last, on 27 December 1949, an independent Indonesia formally came into being and at the 1950 session of the General Assembly, Indonesia was admitted to membership in the United Nations. That the United Nations promoted, rather than obstructed, the birth of a new state in Asia may be said to have enhanced the trust of all Asia in the world organization.

## THE KOREAN WAR

The greatest trial the United Nations has faced has been the Korean War. Since the Korean question had as its background the opposition between the Soviet Union and the United States, the United Nations was placed in an extremely difficult position.

---

7 *Ibid.*, 16th Mtg., 11 Feb. 1946, p. 223.
8 *Ibid.*, 17th Mtg., 12 Feb. 1946, p. 251.

Unlike the League of Nations, which passed through the first decade of its history in relatively peaceful circumstances only to receive an almost mortal blow through the outbreak of the Manchurian Incident, the United Nations was compelled from the beginning to meet a series of difficulties and therefore may be said to have been able to solidify its own foundations through its early trials.

It is well known that there were divergent views as to whether the United Nations action in Korea was justified. But the important point is that the United Nations handling of the Korean War was at each stage supported by an overwhelming majority of its members. This was true even prior to the outbreak of the hostilities. The original General Assembly decision of 14 November 1947 to observe elections in Korea was adopted by a large majority.[9] There was less support for the decision of the Interim Committee of the General Assembly that elections could be held in South Korea only,[10] but the subsequent resolution of 12 December 1948 recognizing the Republic of Korea as the only legitimate government in Korea was approved by a large majority.[11] Subsequently, the application of the Republic of Korea for membership in the United Nations was supported by nine members of the Security Council but vetoed by the USSR.[12] (On the other hand, the Soviet proposal that the Council consider North Korea's application for membership was rejected by a vote of eight to two with one abstention.[13])

After the outbreak of the Korean War, the initial emergency measures adopted by the Security Council and other United Nations policies regarding the Korean situation were approved by large majorities. This may be cited as powerful proof that the United

---

9 Resolution 112(II) was adopted by a vote of 43 to 0, with 6 abstentions.
10 The vote was 31 in favor, 2 against, with 11 members either abstaining or absent from the meeting.
11 Resolution 195(III) was adopted by a vote of 48 to 6, with 1 abstention.
12 S.C.O.R., 4th Yr., No. 26, 423rd Mtg., 8 Apr. 1949, p. 15.
13 *Ibid.*, No. 13, 410th Mtg., 16 Feb. 1949, p. 15.

Nations has substantial prestige over and beyond its merely formalistic effectiveness.

The action the United Nations took regarding the Korean War is a highly valuable precedent. For the first time ample justice was done to the *raison d'être* of the United Nations as a world peace organization. Holding that the invasion of the Republic of Korea by the North Korean troops constituted a breach of the peace, the Security Council adopted a resolution calling for the immediate cessation of hostilities and the withdrawal of North Korean troops. This resolution was approved on 25 June 1950 by a vote of nine in favor and one abstention (Yugoslavia), the Soviet Union being absent from the meeting.[14] Two days later the Security Council adopted a resolution recommending that the United Nations members assist the Republic of Korea to repel the armed attack by North Korea.[15] Only Yugoslavia voted against this recommendation; two members, Egypt and India, failed to receive instructions from their governments in time and did not participate in the voting. Later the Indian delegate expressed his government's approval of the resolution and the Egyptian delegate announced that his government would have abstained from voting. The absence of the Soviet delegate from the Council's meetings when these resolutions were adopted gave rise to theoretical as well as practical questions. But the fact remains that the Security Council by a large majority concluded that there was a breach of the peace and recommended that member nations take forcible measures for dealing with this situation. Eventually (after the resolution of 7 July) sixteen member countries joined in military action under a unified command. Thus, while the League of Nations was unable to take effective sanctions against aggression, the United Nations has been able to do so. It, therefore, is a great improvement over its predecessor as a world peace organization.

---

[14] S.C.O.R., 5th Yr., No. 15, 473rd Mtg., 25 June 1950, pp. 7-8, 13-14, and 18.
[15] *Ibid.*, No. 17, 474th Mtg., 27 June 1950, pp. 4 and 16.

While the functioning of the United Nations was seriously hampered from the outset by the Soviet exercise of its veto in the Security Council, the Korean War gave rise to an effort to compensate for this shortcoming. On 2 November 1950 the General Assembly, by an overwhelming majority of 52 to 5, adopted the "Uniting for Peace" resolution.[16] While the General Assembly has thereby been strengthened, this does not mean that it can take over the functions envisaged in the Charter for the Security Council. It cannot therefore ensure international peace and security. The Security Treaty between the United States and Japan, for instance, implies that the treaty is needed precisely because, under the present circumstances, the United Nations is unable to take adequate measures for preserving international peace and security.[17] However, from the Japanese viewpoint, it may be expected that with the adoption of the "Uniting for Peace" resolution, the world organization can, through a resolution by the General Assembly, take proper measures to assist Japan if it becomes the object of a clear-cut aggression.

The view is widely held that the United Nations action in Korea was valid and that the world organization discharged its function as a guardian of peace and security (even though it was not completely successful in its endeavors). There are those who consider that its actions were unjust and who take a pessimistic view of the capacity of the United Nations to maintain peace and security. In the first place, according to them, the Korean War was a civil disturbance; the issue should have been left to the decision of the

---

[16] Resolution 377(V). For further discussion of this resolution, see above, pp. 113 ff.

[17] Article IV states that the treaty "shall expire whenever . . . there shall have come into force such United Nations arrangements . . . as will satisfactorily provide for the maintenance . . . of international peace and security in the Japan Area." Raymond Dennett and Katherine D. Durant (eds.), *Documents on American Foreign Relations* (Princeton: Published for World Peace Foundation by Princeton University Press, 1953), Vol. XIII, 1951, p. 267.

Korean people; and therefore the United Nations hasty conclusion that there was a breach of international peace was rash and erroneous. Secondly, the nations which support the United States were able by their sheer numerical strength to outvote the Soviet bloc and ignore its wishes. The Soviet bloc, which comprises one-third of the total population of the world, had at that time only five votes in the United Nations. Thirdly, it is contended that the People's Republic of China entered the Korean War with its "volunteer army" because the United States associated the Korean War with the Formosa problem and that the United Nations, in branding the People's Republic of China as an aggressor, made the settlement of the situation difficult.

There are arguments both pro and con regarding the United Nations action in the Korean War, but at least the following three points are generally recognized: (1) While there is some room for doubt as to the sense in which the Korean War was a breach of the peace, the fact that the United Nations reached this conclusion and the recommendation it made for action by the member states make the Korean War the first occasion in which a world peace body has acted in such a manner. It signifies that the international organization has developed to the stage where it can take such action. (2) The Korean War remained a local war because the wishes of the world for peace were unified through the United Nations. The great value of the role the world organization played becomes clear when we consider how much worse the situation could have been, had it not been for the United Nations. (3) The opposition of East and West reached its peak in the Korean War and in this situation the Arab-Asian states acted as a buffer. Many of the proposals by the Arab-Asian states for settling the Korean War were rejected, but it cannot be denied that they did win considerable support and acted as a sort of check on both of the opposing camps. At the seventh session of the General Assembly, for example, the Indian proposal concerning the problem of repatriating the prisoners of war was approved by a vote of 54 to 5 (the Soviet bloc) and 1 abstention (Nationalist China).[18] Although neither the Peking nor North Korean governments accepted this proposal, the truce agreement finally reached on 27 July 1953 was substantially in accord with this Indian plan. It must be admitted that the unity of the East Asian and Arab states, with India as the central force, had an important effect upon the situation. The contribution which these states made at various points in the handling of the Korean conflict is significant evidence of the world-wide character of the United Nations.

[18] See General Assembly Resolution 610(VII), 3 Dec. 1952.

*chapter twelve*

# Japan's Security and the United Nations

Japan's great interest in the United Nations has centered on a desire to provide for the country's security. Having under its Constitution abolished armaments and renounced the right of war, Japan has looked to the United Nations to guarantee its security. At the same time, since the United Nations is the most important international organization for the maintenance of peace and security, Japan is interested in giving the Organization whatever possible support it can.

Is the United Nations, then, fully capable of maintaining peace and security? More specifically, is it capable of providing for Japan's security? It is open to question whether the United Nations is really capable of doing so. The Japanese people have some anxieties on this point. Thus far, their confidence has been influenced by the manner in which the United Nations has acted when an international conflict has occurred or when international peace has been threatened, and by the extent to which these actions have been successful. When the action was ineffectual, there was a tendency for the Japanese to be indifferent to the United Nations and to remain neutral, to keep apart from world conflict and to avoid becoming involved. When the United Nations has taken effective action, there has been a feeling of trust in the Organization and a desire to seek security through the United Nations.

As the initial chapters of this study clearly indicate, the problem of Japan's security has been the underlying motif in the discussions on the United Nations in the Japanese Diet and in the press. A brief summary of the course of this debate is included here as a background to the consideration of three issues of particular importance to Japan: (1) Is "permanent neutrality" a desirable or practical policy for Japan? (2) Should Japan participate in possible enforcement actions taken by the United Nations? (3) Under what conditions should Japan enter into a collective security arrangement for the Pacific area?

## THE DEBATE ON SECURITY AND NEUTRALITY

The attitude of Japan toward the United Nations is based upon a desire to obtain a guarantee of Japan's security through the United Nations. The Japanese government has steadily adhered to this policy and it has generally been supported by public opinion. At times, there have been opposing arguments but, on the whole, the basic attitude has been to seek security through the United Nations.

From the end of the war to the middle of 1946, under the occupation policies enforced by the Allied powers, Japan had no voice in international affairs and did not express a clear attitude concerning the United Nations. Yet, the opinion was widely held that Japan could place its trust in the United Nations in view of the fact that the great powers were co-operating in the United

Nations. There was general confidence in the Organization and an anticipation that it would guarantee world security. This amounted to a belief that Japanese security would be guaranteed by the United Nations.

As the opposition between the great powers became sharper, confidence in the United Nations decreased. There was still a belief in the United Nations and a general hope for its success; however, with the frequent exercise of the veto, greater dissatisfaction came to be expressed. Thus while the Japanese public still hoped that the United Nations could guarantee the peace of the world, at the same time there was dissatisfaction with the failure of the Organization to achieve expected results.

From the beginning of 1949 to the outbreak of the Korean War, there was a strong tendency in Japan to insist on a policy of neutrality. A major impetus to this development was the statement by General MacArthur in March 1949 that the United States wished Japan to be "the Switzerland of the Pacific." By this time the conflict between the United States and the USSR had become serious; the world was divided into two blocs; and the United Nations was not living up to the hopes previously held for it. The Japanese grew more apprehensive as to just how much they could rely on the United Nations and, under the circumstances, the idea of neutrality, especially permanent neutrality, spread quickly.

Confronted by a tendency for the government to favor co-operation with the United States, and possibly a regional security arrangement, the opposition parties insisted on a neutral policy. The Communist party and the Workers and Farmers party (the ultra-leftish political parties) wanted closer relations with the USSR and Communist China and supported the stand of neutrality because it would be advantageous to the Communist nations. The Socialist party, for different reasons, supported neutrality because it did not favor a regional arrangement, such as a Pacific pact, which implied dependence on the United States. Its attitude was also based on its opposition to capitalism.

Moreover, as Japan had little experience in international relations, the people were not fully aware of the fact that neutrality was neither appropriate nor possible in the existing international situation. During this period the editorials in the leading newspapers, as a general rule, supported neutrality. Many intellectuals, and the leading magazines especially, also advocated a policy of neutrality. There were many who even insisted that Japan should not enter the United Nations. Among the intellectuals, there were a few who argued that neutrality was not appropriate, theoretically or practically, as a means for security. Moreover, the government consistently favored joining the United Nations. If the United Nations could not provide adequate security, the government favored a regional arrangement or an agreement with a particular nation to establish security.

When the North Korean Army launched its aggressive military action, many Japanese discovered that neutrality without military power was just a paper plan, merely impractical idealism. Not only that, there was a strong tendency toward relying on the United Nations now that the Organization had demonstrated that it could act quickly to stop aggression.

From this time on, the argument that Japan should seek security through the United Nations became strong, and the neutrality argument receded. Among the reasons for this was that the acts of aggression by the North Koreans with the support of the USSR, and the vigorous reaction of the free nations under the leadership of the United States, brought into the open the opposition between the United States and the USSR. With this development, trust in the United Nations was strengthened due to the fact that it acted promptly and took effective measures to suppress the aggressor. Thus, while the neutrality argument weakened, trust in the United Nations increased, and there was strong feeling in favor of seeking Japan's security through the United Nations.

Editorials in the leading newspapers stated that it was possible for the United Nations to ensure the security of Japan. There were many intellectuals who expressed the same opinion. The government's attitude reflected the same tendencies. The government had always advocated security through the United Nations and this position was strengthened at the time of the Korean War.

Later, when the Chinese Communist forces intervened in the Korean War, there was some criticism of the United Nations among writers and thinkers in Japan. Confidence in the Organization decreased somewhat, not because the United Nations forces had to retreat before the Chinese forces, but because of the long delay in branding Communist China as an aggressor. It was argued that the United Nations was taking a compromising attitude toward a big power. Dissatisfaction with this wavering attitude was expressed and there was some anxiety as to whether the United Nations would be effective in guaranteeing Japan's security. However, when the United Nations decided in February 1951 to censure Communist China, trust in the Organization was again expressed.

The Korean incident was the turning point; after that support for the United Nations continued to increase and the arguments for neutralism were on the wane, although they did not quite disappear. There was some revival of the "neutrality debate" at the time of the conclusion of the Japanese Peace Treaty and the Japan-United States Security Treaty. Some opposed Japan's signing the Peace Treaty on the ground that it would mean allying Japan with one of the two worlds, which would be inconsistent with a stand of neutrality. The Left Wing Socialist party took this attitude. However, few in the general public opposed the Peace Treaty. There was stronger opposition to the Security Treaty between Japan and the United States, as it would clearly mean a connection with one of the two worlds. For instance, the Right Wing Socialist party was for the Peace Treaty but against the Security Treaty. However, Japan as a nation and as a people supported both the Peace Treaty and Security Treaty.

It may be concluded that as a general policy Japan has always sought security through the United Nations. There have been at times opposing tendencies, but the basic attitude has remained the same. The policy of the government has been unchanged. During the initial period of occupation, this attitude was not put in so many words, but merely intimated. Later the government expressed its policy more clearly and after the Korean War there was little question as to the government's position. With the signing of the Peace Treaty in September 1951, the hope of Japan's entering the United Nations was clearly voiced and Japan promised that it would act in accordance with the purposes and principles of the United Nations.

The general attitude of the public has been that Japan should join the United Nations and seek security through it. Although the neutrality argument held sway for a time, it lost its strength. Among the students and organized workers there still are a considerable number who support it. In this connection, there has been some reference to Austria's status of permanent neutrality. When Austria was admitted to the United Nations on 14 December 1955, some scholars expressed the view that Japan might follow this example. This idea found support particularly among those people who had favored permanent neutrality for Japan.

The members of the Study Group unanimously agreed that Japanese security must be sought through the United Nations. It was recognized that other measures would also be necessary and the dominant opinion was that, under the present international situation, some sort of regional arrangement would be necessary. However, this would be only supplementary to the United Nations, and the basic principle would be security through the United Nations. A neutral policy was not supported by even a single member of the special Study Group.

## THE ARGUMENT AGAINST "PERMANENT NEUTRALITY"

In view of the importance that the idea of "permanent neutrality" attained in Japan, it would seem worthwhile to state the reasons why the members of the Study Group concluded that such a policy would not be a proper means for ensuring Japan's security.

A policy of neutrality was possible in the days when international society was less fully developed, and war was a matter of interest only to the parties concerned. When traffic and trade among nations were not brisk, and the nations were more or less self-sufficient, wars did not greatly affect other nations. They could maintain a position of neutrality. As international society has developed, and traffic and trade among nations has increased, wars have come to have a great influence on other nations and have become a problem seriously affecting all their interests. For instance, in time of war international transportation, trade, and cultural exchange are seriously hampered, almost to the point where they can no longer be carried out. Moreover, if a stronger nation starts a war in order to take over the territory or resources of a weaker nation, the international order breaks down and international security is endangered. War can no longer be a matter of indifference even to those nations that do not directly participate. They cannot and should not stand aside, assume a position of neutrality, and merely watch the progress of the war. They should try to prevent the war. In particular, when a nation starts an aggressive war, all nations should co-operate to repress it.

This concept was inherent in the League of Nations Covenant, Article 11 of which stated:

> Any war, or threat of war, whether immediately affecting any of the members of the League or not, is hereby declared a matter of concern to the whole League, and the League shall take any action that may be deemed wise and effectual to safeguard the peace of nations.

Thus, the League recognized clearly that war was a matter of international concern and that the League should itself take steps to prevent it. This same concept is present in the United Nations system. Indeed, the United Nations Charter specifies even more drastic measures for dealing with threats to peace and acts of aggression. Furthermore, Article 2, paragraph 5, of the Charter stipulates: "All Members shall give the United Nations every assistance in any action it takes in accordance with the present Charter . . ." With the development of international society and the close relationships among the nations, the concept of neutrality cannot be justified, even theoretically. All the nations should co-operate for the prevention of war.

Moreover, neutrality is virutally impossible in practice. Modern warfare tends to become worldwide in scope, not only because of the large-scale methods employed but also because of the extremely close relations among nations. Actually, the First World War involved thirty-three nations either as participants or "associated" powers. A number of nations, such as Spain and the Scandinavian countries, remained neutral; others, such as Belgium and Luxembourg, attempted to do so, but when Germany violated their neutrality, they became involved in the war. An even larger number of nations were involved in the Second World War. In the final stages, close to sixty nations were involved. Very few countries found it possible to remain "neutral" and again many that wished to do so were attacked by the warring nations or became involved in the war by other means. In the present-day world, neutrality is very difficult to maintain and there is a strong possibility of all nations being involved in a war, whethei they like it or not. It must be concluded that neutrality, or permanent neutrality, is practically impossible.

A further argument against permanent neutrality is that such a policy would be incompatible with membership in the United Nations. This is clear from the provisions of the United Nations Charter, particularly Articles 1(1), 2(5), and 4(1). At the San Francisco Conference, France proposed that Article 2(5) specifically state that no nation could avail itself of the status of neutrality to escape from its obligations under the Charter. The French delegate explained that the proposal referred to "permanent neutrality." However, the proposal was withdrawn because it was felt that such a provision was unnecessary since it was obvious that a position of neutrality was incompatible with membership in the United Nations.[1]

Those favoring "permanent neutrality" have made much of the special position of Japan. Because of the provisions in the Constitution for the renunciation of war and abolition of armaments, it is argued that Japan is unable to participate in any enforcement action and therefore can only follow a position of neutrality. But enforcement action is not necessarily military action, and even when military measures are necessary, all nations are not called upon to provide forces or to participate in militaiy action. There are non-military measures that the United Nations can take, and even those nations without military power can very well participate in them. However, if it does so, a country can no longer be neutral for neutrality is a position in which a state gives no assistance to warring nations. A nation undertaking to participate in non-military measures may be called upon to sever economic and diplomatic relations with the nation responsible for aggression or for a breach of the peace, and to give assistance, economic or otherwise, to the nation attacked. Thus the nation participating in non-military measures cannot maintain an impartial attitude toward the warring countries; it can no longer be neutral. It is possible for unarmed Japan to participate in non-military measures, and in that case Japan would not be neutral. Thus, the strictures in the Constitution, Japan's lack of armaments, and its subsequent inability to participate fully in enforcement measures cannot be considered adequate grounds for insisting on a policy of permanent neutrality.

For the above reasons, it may be concluded that a neutral policy is inappropriate and that Japan should co-operate with other nations through the United Nations for general security.

---

[1] *Documents of the United Nations Conference on International Organization, San Francisco, 1945* (New York: United Nations Information Organizations, 1945), Vol. VI, pp. 400-01.

## PARTICIPATION IN UNITED NATIONS ENFORCEMENT ACTION

As indicated above, because of Japan's renunciation of war, abolition of armaments, and rejection of the right of belligerency, there is some question whether Japan is in a position to participate in enforcement actions either through the United Nations or under regional mutual assistance arrangements. It would be natural for Japan to participate in enforcement action through the United Nations, but there is some doubt as to the exact method of such participation.

The belief that Japan should participate to the extent compatible with its special position is based upon a recognition of the importance of co-operation among nations for the maintenance of international peace and security. The interests of all nations are directly involved in the maintenance of international peace and security which not only should be achieved through co-operation but can only be achieved by co-operation. Before international society was fully developed, nations could still be self-sufficient, at least to a certain extent. Problems of war and peace did not necessarily concern all nations. However, as international society has developed and nations have exercised a greater influence on each other culturally, economically, and politically, war has come to have serious consequences for all nations. In the present world, all wars and threats of war are matters of concern to all nations.

This was clearly recognized at the time the League of Nations was established. The implication of Article 11 of the Covenant (quoted above)[2] was that, irrespective of whether a particular member was at war or not, or indeed even if none of the members of the League was directly involved in a war, it should still be a matter of great concern to the whole League. Until that time, war was considered merely a matter of interest to the parties involved;

---

[2] See p. 203.

other nations could maintain a position of "neutrality." However, as this provision of the League Covenant made clear, even nations not participating in a war had an interest in it and could not remain neutral. This was a basic change in the attitude of nations toward war. If this was true at the time of the League of Nations, it is even more true today. There is more reason for the United Nations to take the position that all wars and threats of war are a matter of interest to all the members of the United Nations irrespective of whether the member nation is directly involved.

Accordingly, every nation in the world must co-operate to prevent war and the threat of war; international peace and security must be maintained through the co-operation of all nations. This, too, was clearly recognized in the Covenant of the League of Nations, which declared that "the League shall take any action that may be deemed wise and effectual to safeguard the peace of nations." This meant that in the final analysis all the members of the League should take concerted measures to maintain peace.

Similarly, under the United Nations Charter wars and threats of war are matters of concern to all the members and the United Nations must take adequate and effective measures to deal with them. According to the Charter, the United Nations is to take "effective and collective measures" for the maintenance of international peace and security, and all members are enjoined to give the United Nations every assistance in such actions.

It would be natural for Japan to adhere to this principle and give all possible assistance to the United Nations in measures it takes for the maintenance of peace and security. This is the basic responsibility of a United Nations member. If a nation refused to accept this responsibility, that is, refused to participate in enforcement action and took a position of neutrality, it would not be qualified to be a member of the United Nations. This was clearly understood at the San Francisco Conference and it is for this very reason that Switzerland, which maintains a position of permanent neutrality, has not entered the United Nations. It is the primary and basic obligation of the member nations to participate in collective measures for peace and security and to give all possible assistance to actions by the United Nations. As a member of the United Nations, Japan should, as a matter of course, fulfil this responsibility.

There are many measures which the United Nations may take by way of enforcement action, including non-military action as mentioned in Article 41 of the Charter, and military measures as in Article 42. With regard to the latter, the members of the United Nations are supposed to provide armed forces, facilities, or other forms of assistance. This may include the use of airfields, ports or other bases, and the offer of material, labor, transportation, and other assistance. All members of the United Nations would not be called upon to participate equally in all enforcement actions. The decision should be made according to the circumstances of the respective nations. Therefore, even if, as a general principle, Japan is to participate in United Nations enforcement measures, this does not necessarily mean that Japan would participate in all of these actions. It is quite possible to join in only some of them.

It would be preferable for Japan to participate in enforcement actions by means other than the contribution of military forces. These means should include not only participation in non-military measures, but also the offering of facilities and other forms of assistance. The majority of the Japanese people support this idea. Actually, during the Korean conflict, Japan co-operated to a considerable extent with the United Nations, contributing both facilities and assistance. This co-operation was initiated while Japan was still occupied by the Allied forces, and was not in the position to resist their demands. But this was not the only reason; Japan recognized that the United Nations was endeavoring to maintain peace and, therefore, co-operation was considered appropriate and natural. The majority of the Japanese think that it would be equally natural for Japan to co-operate with the United Nations in giving assistance and facilities in the future.

Although there are some who oppose this idea, their number is not great. They think Japan should take a neutral stand in the event of a war among other nations, even if the conflict results from aggression or a breach of the peace by one nation, and consequent enforcement action by other nations. These people do not recognize the difference between a nation resorting to aggressive action which is no less than an international crime, and a nation joining in enforcement measures which have the character of an international police action. They do not understand the new and basic characteristics of United Nations enforcement measures but look upon war as a return to former times and oppose participation in it.

On the question whether Japan should contribute military forces to a United Nations enforcement action, opinion is sharply divided. The arguments pro and con are almost equally influential. The Study Group found itself evenly divided on this issue. Those who are against Japan's participation in United Nations military measures stress the special situation of Japan: the Constitutional provisions for the renunciation of war, the abolition of armaments, and the denial of the right of belligerency. They argue that Japan cannot have regular armed forces and cannot therefore co-operate by offering to contribute forces to any United Nations action.

At present, there exist in Japan lightly equipped forces, known as self-defense forces, but their existence is objected to by some Japanese as a violation of the Constitution. Even if their existence is recognized as a *fait accompli*, it is argued that they are solely for the defense of the nation, or for maintaining security within the nation, and are not to be dispatched abroad in the event of war among other nations.

The arguments against Japan's contributing forces to the United Nations are closely related to the arguments against rearmament. Not only the provisions of the Constitution, but the sentiments of the Japanese people, are stressed in this connection. The Japanese people distrust armed forces. The opinion is widely held that armed forces imply war, that they are not for the defense of the nation but may involve Japan in a war with foreign countries. This results from past experiences. In particular, after the Manchurian Incident, Japanese armed forces were constantly used not for purposes of defense but to carry out an aggressive policy against foreign countries. Japan was not attacked by foreign countries but invited war in its pursuit of foreign territory and natural resources. Therefore, many Japanese cannot get rid of the idea that Japanese forces might be used again to attack other nations. Having fully experienced the miseries of war, they wish to avoid a war as far as possible and there is strong feeling against maintaining any armed forces capable of making war. Japan's past policies are responsible for this distrust.

Another objection to Japanese rearmament is that the possession of armed forces might invite an attack from foreign nations. It is believed that the very existence of armed forces may be considered an expression of hostility against a certain foreign nation which might lead to an attack. Specifically, it is the Communist nations from which Japan is in danger of being attacked. It is argued that, if Japan has no armed forces, it would be obvious that it had no hostile designs on these nations; it would be favorably regarded by these nations and would not be attacked. This idea must be said to be very naive in the present international situation, but however naive it may be, it is supported by many Japanese whose knowledge and experience in international relations are still immature.

Those who oppose Japan's contributing armed forces to the United Nations also argue that the United Nations has no need for such forces. They hold the view that the major powers should offer the main fighting forces for any enforcement action and that the small nations need not necessarily contribute armed forces. This may be said to be one of the basic assumptions of the United Nations itself, as was evident in the report of the United Nations Military Staff Committee concerning the special agreements provided for in Article 43 of the Charter. This report, submitted to the Security Council in April 1947,[3] consisted of 41 articles; on 25 of them the committee members were in agreement. Opinions differed so strongly on the other points that the report was not adopted by the Council. Its contents therefore have no legal validity; but since the points agreed on reflected the opinions of all the Big Five and other nations represented on the Security Council, they can actually be regarded as indicating the approach of the United Nations at that time. One point of agreement was on Article 9, which stated that all the member nations were to have the opportunity and obligation to place armed forces, facilities, and assistance at the disposal of the Security Council. Article 10, however, provided that, at least initially, the permanent members of the Security Council would contribute the major part of the forces, with those from other nations added as they became available. Article 14 stipulated that the contributions by nations other than permanent members need not take the form of armed forces.

In general, it would seem that the permanent members of the Security Council, i. e., the big powers, were to supply the bulk of the armed forces. Whatever forces the other nations contributed would be of a secondary nature, and would be added to the forces already supplied by the big powers. Actually the difference in capabilities of big powers as compared to the small nations is so great that small fighting units from the smaller nations would not prove very effective. Armed forces to be used at the time of an enforcement action should be supplied predominantly by the big powers, with the small nations providing facilities or other assistance where necessary. In view of the above, it would not be inappropriate for Japan to co-operate by giving only assistance and facilities, without offering armed forces. As Japan is a small nation and at present its self-defense forces are only lightly equipped, it has a special reason for not joining in United Nations enforcement action

[3] Security Council, Official Records: 2nd Yr., Special Supple. No. 1, Report of the Military Staff Ctte.

by offering armed forces. The United Nations should take these special reasons into consideration and ask Japan to co-operate with the offer of facilities and assistance.

On the other hand, it may be desirable that all members of the United Nations, even the smallest, offer a certain number of armed forces to express the co-operation of all members. This would demonstrate that all the nations are participating in the enforcement action, not because their own contribution will be militarily significant, but mainly for the political effect. In this sense, there would be some purpose in having even the small nations offer armed forces, however few in number.

Those who feel that Japan should contribute armed forces to any United Nations enforcement action stress the point that peace and security can only be maintained with the co-operation of all nations. They point out that the maintenance of peace and security is the most important problem in international society. They insist that Japan should fully co-operate with the United Nations as a matter of course, and that even though there is no regular army, the defense forces which Japan does possess should be used to co-operate with the United Nations. Some people even go beyond that point and insist that in order for Japan to co-operate fully with the United Nations, the Constitution should be revised to permit the development of regular armed forces.

The necessity for all nations to co-operate for the prevention of war and the maintenance of peace was strongly emphasized at the meetings of the Study Group by Mr. Naotake Sato (former Ambassador to France and Russia, Speaker of the House of Councillors after the end of the war, present member of House of Councillors, and President of the United Nations Association of Japan). He maintained:

> We must develop the idea that the people of the world share the same fate, and that the peace and security of the world must be maintained by the co-operation of all nations. It is necessary to inspire the nations to move in this direction.

> Since Japan is to be under the protection of the United Nations, it is only natural for us to co-operate with the United Nations for the maintenance of international peace and security. It is a selfish and wrong idea for a nation to expect protection from the United Nations, if it is not willing to contribute to it. On this point, it is my opinion that the Japanese Constitution itself must be revised. The preamble of the Constitution stipulates that the existence and security of Japan shall be dependent on the justice and faith of peace-loving nations, but this Constitution was adopted when co-operation among the great powers seemed possible and when it was expected that through their co-operation the peace and security of the world would be secure. However, the international situation has basically changed since that time, and the Constitution must be revised to fit the new situation. In other words, since the original expectation was not fulfilled, Japan should now build up armaments in order to defend the country and to co-operate with the United Nations. This is necessary not only for Japan, but for the United Nations as well.

Other members of the Study Group stressed the point that it would not be inconsistent with the Constitution, or the basic anti-war sentiments of the Japanese people, for Japan to contribute armed forces to an enforcement action undertaken by the United Nations. Mr. Masamichi Royama (formerly Professor at Tokyo University and now President of Ochanomizu Women's University) insisted that:

> It would not be inappropriate for Japan to co-operate with the United Nations with armed forces. While some Japanese strongly object to dispatching Japanese forces abroad, I, personally, am not necessarily against sending them to assist the United Nations or for mutual assistance based on regional security arrangements. We must avoid entering a war again. Not only have we in the Constitution renounced war and denied ourselves the right of belligerency, but the Japanese people feel that they have had enough of war. This common sentiment must be respected. If Japanese armed forces are dispatched abroad to participate in enforcement action under

> the United Nations, or a regional security arrangement, the people, whose sentiments are so universally anti-war, must be made to understand the necessity for this action. If an adequate explanation can be provided, I am not necessarily against the dispatching of our forces abroad.

On this point, another member of the Study Group, Mr. Kisaburo Yokota (Professor of International Law, Tokyo University) stated:

> If we must give an explanation, it might be as follows: The right of belligerency which was renounced in the Japanese Constitution applies to belligerency in a war that is brought about by the conflict of interests of two nations or several nations. Wars were formerly all of this kind, that is, they were conflicts of the armed forces of individual nations, much resembling disputes among individuals. They were, so to speak, private wars. In this kind of war the rights of belligerency were of some importance. However, enforcement action by the United Nations is of an entirely different nature. It is taken in the event that a certain nation breaches the peace or commits an aggressive action and it is directed toward preventing aggression or restoring the peace. Therefore, a United Nations enforcement action amounts to a police action, an international police action, which is by its nature similar to a domestic police action. It is not a belligerent action and as such has no bearing on the right of belligerency as mentioned in the Japanese Constitution.
>
> The term "war" in fact, is not used in the Charter of the United Nations; it mentions threats to the peace, breaches of the peace and acts of aggression and speaks of "collective measures" or "enforcement action." There are various explanations for this usage. In the first place, the Covenant of the League of Nations narrowly defined the circumstances in which a nation could justifiably resort to war. Later the Kellogg-Briand Pact of 1928 outlawed war in general. As a result, nations resorting to actions which were actually war, in the former sense, evaded the use of the term, referring merely to "military action" or "the exercise of the right of self-defense." If one nation called the action "war," then there would have been a clear violation of the Kellogg-Briand Pact.

Thus, in order to evade invocation of the Pact, other phrases were used. The most notable examples of this were the military actions taken by Japan first in Manchuria and later in China proper. In these cases, extensive fighting took place, and they were in actual fact "wars." Japan maintained, however, that these were not wars but merely military action in self-defense.

It should also be noted that traditionally the nation embarking on an aggressive war and the nation resorting to military measures to defend itself were both considered belligerents. No distinction was made between the two. This was extremely unjust, as the nation carrying on the aggressive action was clearly violating international law, while the nation defending itself against an aggression was acting in accordance with international law. Nevertheless, both were formerly treated as warring nations with equal status. The Covenant of the League of Nations and the United Nations Charter provide for sanctions against a nation breaching the peace and carrying out aggressive action. These sanctions are in the nature of a police action to maintain order in international society. Thus wars cease to be private affairs. To clarify this point, the United Nations Charter calls an action to maintain or to restore peace and security an "enforcement action" and evades the use of the word "war," and uses instead such terms as "breaches of the peace," "acts of aggression" and "enforcement action."

Accordingly, when the United Nations takes an enforcement action, it would not be a war in the former sense but an international police action, and if Japan participates in it through offering armed forces, this would not mean participation in a war, but rather participation in an action to prevent war. Japan would not thereby be exercising the right of belligerency, but would be co-operating in the exercise of an international police right. There would be no violation of the Japanese Constitution, notwithstanding the fact that the Constitution does not recognize the right of belligerency. Furthermore, since United Nations enforcement action is not considered to be war, but a police action to prevent war, Japan's participation would not be contradictory to the strong anti-war sentiments of the Japanese people.

> These same considerations would apply in regard to mutual assistance based on regional security arrangements. In this case if a nation party to a regional arrangement is the victim of an aggressive action or attack, the other nations are expected to co-operate in meeting the attack. This again is nothing but a police action for the maintenance of peace and security in the area. It is not a war in the traditional sense. Therefore, participation in it is not participation in a war, nor does it constitute an exercise of the right of belligerency, as specified in the Japanese Constitution. It is participation in the exercise of a regional police right.

The following conclusions may be drawn from this discussion on Japan's possible participation in United Nations enforcement actions. Japan should refrain as far as possible from contributing armed forces on the ground that (1) the Japanese Constitution has abolished armaments and denied the right of belligerency, (2) the people of Japan are strongly opposed to any warlike measures, and (3) the primary responsibility for contributing forces to military enforcement action by the United Nations rests with the great powers. Should it prove desirable for the small nations to offer fighting forces as a demonstration of the unanimous character of enforcement action by the United Nations to prevent wars, it would not be inappropriate for Japan to dispatch a small unit of armed forces. As such an action would not constitute "war" but rather an international police action, it would not be contradictory to the Constitution for Japan to contribute military forces. As to offering facilities and assistance other than armed forces, Japan should fully co-operate with the United Nations and comply with its requests.

## REGIONAL SECURITY ARRANGEMENTS

Although the ideal solution to Japan's security problem would be for the United Nations to guarantee Japan's security, under existing circumstances the United Nations security system is not fully effective. The Japanese people are reluctant to depend solely upon it and feel the necessity for supplementary regional security measures, a need that is recognized by almost all Japanese.

The views of the Study Group concerning the general nature of regional security arrangements and their relation to the United Nations have been set forth in Part Two of this study.[4] Certain special questions arise, however, in connection with the possible participation of Japan in any regional security arrangement. As pointed out, regional security arrangements are based on the right of collective self-defense and provide that, in case of an armed attack, measures will be taken collectively. Any regional security arrangement in which Japan participates should provide that the decision to take collective measures of self-defense against an armed attack be jointly reached by all nations participating in the arrangement, for it is undesirable for nations to decide individually whether or not to exercise the right of collective self-defense. As measures of collective self-defense have important consequences, they should be decided upon by a two-thirds majority of the states concerned, although, since it is likely that measures against an armed attack will have to be taken quickly, the decision might be reached by a simple majority. In any case, the decision should not be left to the individual nations.

Because of Japan's past record of unprovoked aggressive actions taken under the guise of "self-defense," it is especially necessary that any regional security arrangement to which Japan is a party should restrict the right of a nation to resort to armed action on the basis of its own decision. Otherwise, the danger of Japanese aggression in the name of the right of self-defense might again arise. It is true that Japan does not now possess regular armed forces, and even if they are acquired in the future, they are not likely to be powerful. Thus there is little possibility of Japan's taking aggressive armed action of its own accord. Nevertheless, in the light of past

---

[4] See pp. 119 ff.

actions, the people are apprehensive and distrustful of the right of self-defense and are afraid that the government may take unilateral aggressive action, calling it an act of self-defense. If the decision is to be made not by one government but jointly with other nations, this anxiety will be eliminated. It is desirable that the decision be reached jointly by the nations concerned not only in order to alleviate the anxiety and suspicion of the Japanese people but also to demonstrate the co-operation of participating nations in exercising the right of collective self-defense.

Since a regional arrangement in the Pacific area would be primarily designed to insure the security of the Asian nations in that area, the Asian countries in the region should take part in such an arrangement. Some people hold that only Asian states should participate therein. However, since these countries are not at present militarily or economically powerful, a pact among them would not serve as an effective measure for security. Therefore, such a pact might be considered not as an immediate objective but as a future goal. In any case, it is generally agreed that Asian countries in the Pacific must constitute the principal membership in any Pacific pact.

In order to make such a regional arrangement effective, however, the participation of the United States would be necessary. Japan has signed a bilateral security pact with the United States which provides that the security and peace of Japan is to be maintained with the co-operation of the United States. There can, therefore, be no objection by Japan to the participation of the United States in regional arrangements on a wider scale in the Pacific area, should such arrangement be possible.

Any regional arrangement for the Pacific area in which the United States does not participate will not be at all effective. Moreover, since both the United Kingdom and France possess territories in the Pacific, it is necessary to include them in any security arrangement for the area. There seems to be little ground for their exclusion and the arrangements will gain in effectiveness through their participation.

A regional security arrangement in the Pacific area such as described above would not be easy to conclude. There are many obstacles. First, the nations in the area are not closely related with each other; at least, there is no close association as in the case of the nations of the Western hemisphere or Western Europe. In these two areas the nations have extremely close interests—political, social, cultural, and traditional. They share an awareness of the threat to their peace and security, and can therefore take joint measures for co-operative action. An effective regional security arrangement can only be based on close relationships among the nations concerned, but the Asian nations in the Pacific area do not share a common consciousness of social, political, or cultural kinship. It is not easy therefore to sponsor measures for joint action among them.

In particular, the relations between Japan and other Asian countries cannot yet be said to be intimate or friendly. Antagonism toward Japan on the part of those Asian countries that in the past suffered from Japanese aggression is at present still strong. This is evident in the mutual assistance pacts that the United States has concluded with the Philippines and with Australia and New Zealand. While these pacts signify on the one hand an opposition to communism, on the other they are directed toward protecting these countries from a renewal of Japan's past expansionist policies. These nations cannot rid themselves of apprehension regarding the recovery and strengthening of Japan. Therefore, it will not be easy to establish regional arrangements calling for participation by these nations together with Japan. In this regard, participation by a powerful nation like the United States would serve to dissipate the fears of these other nations, for it would then be impossible for Japan to take unilateral action. The other nations might therefore be more receptive to a regional arrangement in the Pacific area.

There is also some opposition in Japan to a regional arrangement for the Pacific area. From the standpoint of its own security, Japan does not stand to gain much from a regional arrangement with

Asian countries. If Japan is attacked, there will be little assistance from other Asian countries. On the other hand, if these countries are attacked, it will be a major burden for Japan to assist them with armed forces. A mutual assistance arrangement with Asian nations would, therefore, be of little profit for Japan. The present Security Treaty between Japan and the United States would be far more effective and, it is argued, there is no need for a further regional arrangement in the Pacific area.

Two main reasons may be advanced to support the argument in favor of substituting a regional security arrangement for the United States-Japan Security Treaty. One is that the bilateral treaty places Japan in a subordinate position, due to the difference in the strengths of the two nations. This is not desirable, and should be avoided if possible. Under a regional arrangement including many nations in the Pacific area, Japan's subordination to the United States would not be so great. Thus, in order to secure real independence for Japan, it is more desirable to rely on a regional security arrangement than on the Security Treaty between Japan and the United States.

The second reason arises from the apprehension and distrust of the Asian countries toward Japan. If Japan relies exclusively on a security pact with the United States, and does not join with the other Asian countries, the distrust and fear of these nations will not only continue but might even increase. Their fear that Japan will get stronger by rearming with United States assistance would be greatly reduced if a regional arrangement, centering around the Asian countries and including Japan, can be made. Many people therefore think it more desirable to have a regional security arrangement in the Pacific area than a security treaty with the United States alone.

It may be said that a regional security arrangement in the Pacific area has about an equal number of supporters and antagonists. The attitude of the government on this subject has not been very clear. In principle it has not opposed regional arrangements but it has taken an ambiguous attitude concerning Japan's participation in such an arrangement. As to the attitudes of the political parties, the conservative parties, which have held the majority in the Diet, have maintained approximately the same attitude as the government. The Right Wing Socialist party, while supporting the United Nations collective security system, has opposed a regional collective security arrangement. It was originally strongly opposed to the Security Treaty between Japan and the United States but this attitude gradually softened and it later approved the treaty in principle, although pressing for some amendments to it. The Left Wing Socialist party maintained its opposition to the Security Treaty and to any regional arrangement, particularly one like NATO. Since the coalition of both wings of the party in 1955, its position has been somewhat fluctuating but more recently it seems to be approaching that of the right wing group.

## SEATO AND JAPAN

The foregoing discussion on regional arrangements goes far to explain Japan's attitude toward the Southeast Asia Treaty Organization, which was set up in 1954 as a regional security arrangement for Southeast Asia. The problem whether Japan should participate in SEATO has seldom been the subject of discussion. Japan has never been invited to join the Organization; however, as the treaty provides that it may be extended by the unanimous agreement of the parties, Japan's membership may possibly become an issue in the future. Neither the Japanese government nor public opinion in general has favored joining SEATO under present conditions. The main reasons for this attitude are as follows: firstly, only three states in Southeast Asia, the Philippines, Thailand, and Pakistan, are parties to SEATO. If it is to be a real regional security organization for Southeast Asia, all the states within that region should be included. It is a fundamental defect of SEATO that a large number of Southeast Asian countries (in particular, Burma, Ceylon, India, and Indonesia) are not members of it. Secondly, Western powers are dominant in SEATO; the United States, the United Kingdom, France, Australia, and New Zealand, are all members, while only three Asian countries have joined it. Furthermore, the Asian members are all small powers, while three of the Western countries are great powers. Thus the Western states are not only in the majority, but their influence in the organization is overwhelming. This may be considered the great defect of SEATO because, if it is to be a regional security organization for Southeast Asia, the countries in that region should form its leading parties.

In addition to these reasons, there are still others that account for the prevailing opinion in Japan against participation in SEATO as it is now constituted. These have been mentioned in the preceding section: the prohibition in the Constitution against the maintenance of armed forces; the anti-war sentiment among the Japanese people; etc.

There are, however, those who hold that in the event all the countries of Scutheast Asia join SEATO, Japan should also participate in it. This opinion is held by a comparatively small number of people, but some of them are well informed and influential. They recognize that the participation of the Western powers is essential for the purpose of building up an effective security organization, but, for SEATO to be a real security organization for Southeast Asia, it is a minimum requirement that it include all the Southeast Asian nations. When this condition is met, they favor Japan's participation in the organization.

In the Study Group in Tokyo, many members shared this view; a few even felt that it was desirable that Japan join SEATO as soon as possible. At the meetings in Osaka and Kobe, a few persons were hesitant in expressing their support for SEATO. However, a majority took the view that if all the nations of Southeast Asia joined SEATO, it would be an appropriate regional security organization for the free nations in Asia, and that, if it should be extended to cover the Northeast Asian region, Japan should be ready to participate in it.

*chapter thirteen*

# Japan's Admission to the United Nations

## JAPAN'S REQUEST FOR ADMISSION

Shortly after the Peace Treaty became effective in 1952, Japan requested admission to the United Nations. At the meeting of the Security Council on 18 September 1952, Japan's application was supported by an overwhelming majority but it was rejected because of the one negative vote by the USSR.[1] On 21 December of the same year, the General Assembly declared that Japan was a peace-loving nation, as defined in Article 4 of the Charter, and was able and willing to carry out its obligations under the Charter. The Assembly considered that Japan should therefore be admitted to the United Nations and requested that the Security Council take

---

[1] Security Council, Official Records (S.C.O.R.): 7th Yr., 602nd Mtg.,18 Sept. 1952, p. 15.

note of this decision.[2] The resolution was adopted by a vote of 50 to 5 with 4 abstentions and 1 absent. The opposition to Japan's admission, as indicated by one negative vote in the Security Council and five in the General Assembly, was almost negligible (particularly when considered in the light of the provisions of the Covenant of the League of Nations by which a two-thirds vote of the Assembly sufficed for the admission of a new member). The fact that Japan's admission to the United Nations was blocked was not only a source of great regret to Japan but also a proof of the grievous defect inherent in the veto system. As pointed out earlier it is unreasonable to recognize the right of veto in questions concerning admission to membership.[3]

In 1953 the question of Japan's admission to the United Nations was again taken up in the General Assembly, together with the applications of many other states. No positive results were obtained. The General Assembly, however, established a Committee of Good Offices (consisting of representatives of Egypt, the Netherlands, and Peru) and empowered it to conduct negotiations with members of the Security Council "with the object of exploring the possibilities of reaching an understanding which would facilitate the admission of new Members."[4] In 1954 the General Assembly again decided to send the pending applications for membership back to the Security Council for "further consideration and positive recommendations" and requested the Committee of Good Offices to continue its efforts.[5] Notwithstanding these resolutions, none of the many states which had applied for membership was admitted. It may be noted, however, that Soviet opposition to Japan's admission was considerably toned down in these years.

---

[2] See General Assembly Resolution 620(VII)B, 21 Dec. 1952, and General Assembly, Official Records (G.A.O.R.): 7th Sess., 410th Plenary Mtg., 21 Dec. 1952, p. 479.

[3] See above, pp. 133-35.

[4] General Assembly Resolution 718(VIII), 23 Oct. 1953.

[5] General Assembly Resolution 817(IX), 23 Nov. 1954.

At the tenth session of the General Assembly in 1955 a strong sentiment developed for the admission of new members. Almost all members urged the necessity and desirability of the widest possible membership for the United Nations, and twenty-eight states joined in proposing a draft resolution requesting the Security Council to consider the "pending applications for membership of all those countries about which no problem of unification arises."[6] This draft resolution, slightly amended, was adopted on 8 December 1955.[7] In the Security Council, China proposed to add the Republic of Korea and the Republic of Vietnam to the list of eighteen countries recommended by the General Assembly. The USSR voted against the admission of the two states proposed by China. China thereupon voted against the admission of Outer Mongolia, which induced the USSR to vote against the admission of fifteen other countries. On the following day, however, the USSR proposed a new draft resolution to admit sixteen countries; Japan and Mongolia were not included. This draft resolution was adopted by the Council on 14 December[8] and the admission of the sixteen new members was approved by the General Assembly on the same date.[9]

This news was received in Japan with infinite regret and much embarrassment. While it was true that Japan was glad that a number of countries had been admitted to the United Nations and that the latter had thereby become a much more universal organization, it was difficult to understand why Japan had been singled out. Why did the USSR choose to couple Japan with Mongolia, which were to be refused membership in the United Nations? The Japanese people could not help feeling that a great injustice had been done.

[6] United Nations Doc. A/AC.80.L.3, 16 Nov. 1955. These countries were: Albania, Austria, Bulgaria, Cambodia, Ceylon, Finland, Hungary, Ireland, Italy, Japan, Jordan, Laos, Libya, Mongolian People's Republic, Nepal, Portugal, Romania, Spain.

[7] General Assembly Resolution 918(X), 8 Dec. 1955. The resolution requested the Security Council to consider the pending applications for membership of all the *eighteen* countries about which there was no problem of unification.

[8] See S.C.O.R., 10th Yr., 701st to 705th Mtgs., 10 to 14 Dec. 1955.

[9] General Assembly Resolution 995(X), 14 Dec. 1955.

Meanwhile, negotiations between Japan and the USSR for the termination of the state of war and resumption of normal diplomatic relations were dragging on. They had begun in June 1955. One of the important topics in the negotiations was Japan's admission to the United Nations. As Soviet opposition was the main obstacle, the Japanese representatives wished to use this occasion to get express consent from the Soviet Union for Japan's admission to the United Nations. This they finally succeeded in doing. A joint declaration by Japan and the USSR, which was signed at last on 19 October 1956, laid down in paragraph 4: "The Union of Soviet Socialist Republics shall support the application by Japan for membership in the United Nations."[10] Thus the greatest obstacle to Japan's admission was removed.

It was expected that Japan's application would be approved at the eleventh session of the General Assembly in 1956, and the Japanese people was extremely gratified to find this expectation fulfilled. At the meeting of the Security Council on 12 December 1956 the representative of Peru presented a resolution recommending approval of Japan's application. All members of the Security Council, including the representative of the USSR, supported the proposal and the resolution was unanimously adopted.[11] In the General Assembly fifty-one states presented a joint resolution for Japan's admission and on 18 December 1956 all the seventy-seven states present voted in its favor.[12] Japan was thereby admitted to the United Nations.

After the voting, Mr. M. Shigemitsu, Deputy Prime Minister and Foreign Minister of Japan, in reply to the many speeches of welcome, made the following statement:

[10] Japanese Ministry of Foreign Affairs, Information Bulletin, Vol. III, No. 21 (official translation by the Ministry).

[11] S.C.O.R., 11th Yr., 756th Mtg., 12 Dec. 1956.

[12] See General Assembly Resolution 1113(XI), 18 Dec. 1956, and G.A.O.R., 11th Sess., 623rd Plenary Mtg., 18 Dec. 1956, p. 723.

The people of Japan today desire peace for all time, and are deeply conscious of the high ideals controlling human relationships. We have determined to preserve our security and existence, trusting in the justice and faith of the peace-loving peoples of the world. We recognize that all peoples of the world have the right to live in peace, free from fear and want. We desire to occupy an honoured place in an international society striving for the preservation of peace and the banishment of tyranny and slavery, oppression and intolerance, for all time from the earth.[13]

. . . .

Japan is gratified that, together with the maintenance of peace, the United Nations places great importance on humanitarianism. It has taken up the problem of disarmament as a major task in the pursuit of its objective of maintaining peace. It is also devoting its efforts to the prohibition of weapons of mass destruction, because of its vital concern for humanity.

Being the only country which has experienced the horrors of the atomic bomb, Japan knows its tragic consequences. It was from the standpoint of humanity that . . . both Houses of the Diet of Japan adopted in February 1956 a resolution calling for the prohibition of the use and testing of nuclear bombs. . . .

We earnestly hope that, under the leadership of the United Nations, the great task of disarmament will be successfully consummated.

. . . .

The basis for peace and progress in Asia is to be found in the economic development of the countries of the region. The countries of Asia today are devoting their full efforts toward their economic advancement. Not a few of them require the further assistance of the United Nations and its Members in order to make their efforts more fruitful. Japan's relations with them are those of mutual co-operation and common

---

[13] This paragraph is based on the Preamble of the postwar Constitution of Japan.

> destiny . . . and it holds great expectations from the growth and development of those countries.
>
> . . . .
>
> The substance of Japan's political, economic and cultural life is the product of the fusion within the last century of the civilizations of the Orient and the Occident. In a way, Japan may well be regarded as a bridge between the East and the West. It is fully conscious of the great responsibilities of such a position.[14]

## JAPAN'S OBJECTIVES IN JOINING THE UNITED NATIONS

The reasons why Japan sought admission to the United Nations and the advantages it hopes to derive therefrom are as follows:

*To provide for Japan's security:* The greatest advantage in joining the United Nations is the security guarantee thereby obtained. This is considered one of the most important motives of all states in joining the United Nations, but it is particularly important for Japan for the special reason that under its postwar Constitution Japan has abolished armaments and renounced the right of belligerency. It is true that at present a degree of *de facto* rearmament is taking place through the build-up of defense forces. However, there are strong objections to these measures in some Japanese circles, and there are various legal obstacles to the formal establishment of an army. Also, for economic and other reasons, it is virtually impossible for Japan to establish armed forces sufficiently strong to defend its own security. The desire that Japan's security be guaranteed by the United Nations is supported by almost all Japanese.

*To contribute to world peace and security through the United Nations:* A second objective in joining the United Nations is that this will enable Japan to contribute its share to world peace and

[14] G.A.O.R., 11th Sess., 623rd Plenary Mtg., 18 Dec. 1956, pp. 727-28.

security as a member of the international community. Such an objective is in accord with the spirit of the new Japanese Constitution.

The Preamble of the Constitution states that Japan is "determined to preserve [its] security and existence, trusting in the justice and faith of the peace-loving people of the world." The United Nations is an organization of peace-loving nations. Relying upon the sense of justice and the good faith of its members, the United Nations attempts, through their co-operation, to maintain peace and security and to realize the development and welfare of the international community. Japan should consider that an important objective of its membership in the United Nations is to participate in the realization of the noble ideals of the Organization by co-operating with other nations in keeping world peace and security, and by contributing to the progress of the international community.

*To solve the social and cultural problems of Japan:* A third advantage which will accrue to Japan through membership in the United Nations is that this will be conducive to solving the social and cultural problems that exist in Japan. Japan lags behind the advanced nations of the West, especially in social and cultural matters. By joining the United Nations, and co-operating with the other nations, Japan can be measurably assisted in solving its own present problems.

The record of Japan's experience with the League of Nations yields many examples of the benefits derived in this regard. In the days of the League of Nations, for instance, the International Labour Organisation adopted various conventions, the provisions of which were fairly advanced in the light of the conditions in Japan at that time. Although their implementation was extremely difficult, Japan, as a member of the League and of the International Labour Organisation, found itself politically and morally obliged to adopt many of these conventions. Japanese ratification was naturally expedited when other member states adopted and ratified these agreements. Ratification induced the legal authorities in Japan to enforce the conventions properly. Membership in the League of

Nations proved extremely helpful in fulfilling these obligations because, when a convention was not heeded, pressure by the League directly or indirectly accelerated its enforcement.

It is worth noting that Japan has been extremely sensitive about maintaining the appearance of a civilized nation, and has always aimed at attaining the general standard maintained by civilized countries. Although Japan occupied a position as one of the leading powers in the League of Nations, this position was based largely on political and military considerations. Frankly speaking, Japan was not among the leading powers from a social and cultural standpoint. At any rate, since Japan was a permanent member of the Council, every effort was made to maintain, socially and culturally, the status of a leading nation and to achieve internationally accepted standards. Therefore, whenever the League of Nations made a case of Japan's low standards, efforts were made to raise the level. Even today, conditions in Japan cannot be regarded as equal to the standards of a first-class nation, but the general desire, especially in official quarters, is not to fall below international levels in the social fields. With regard to general labor conditions in Japan and the working conditions of minors, women, etc., every precaution has been taken to maintain world standards. Should the government itself fail to pay enough attention to these problems, it is nevertheless inclined to respond to public criticism when it is attacked for allowing low standards.

From this standpoint, therefore, membership in the United Nations is considered advantageous for elevating social and cultural standards in Japan as well as for solving related problems. Of course, these questions are not exclusively handled by the United Nations. They are more concretely treated by the specialized agencies of the United Nations and Japan is a member of every one of these agencies. It is obvious, however, that there is great advantage in being a member not only of the individual specialized agencies but also of the United Nations itself which is the mother, so to speak, of these agencies. Furthermore, these problems are often discussed by the United Nations, particularly in the Economic and Social Council, and membership in the United Nations should therefore greatly contribute to improving Japan's standards and solving its social and cultural problems.

In the discussions in the Study Group this point was emphasized particularly by those concerned with social and cultural problems. For instance, Miss Taki Fujita, Director of the Women's and Minors' Bureau, Ministry of Labor, stressed that membership in the United Nations would contribute to the solution of the problems of minors and the improvement of the status of women. Mr. Tamon Maeda, who was a delegate to the International Labour Organisation in the days of the League of Nations, emphasized the necessity and benefit of Japan's joining the United Nations in order to improve labor conditions.

*To co-operate in the solution of social and cultural problems of Asian nations:* Membership in the United Nations is considered of value for Japan not only for the purpose of solving its own social and cultural problems, but also in order to co-operate with other nations, especially the nations of Asia, in coping with their similar problems. Although Japan cannot in many respects be called an advanced nation, in contrast to other Asian nations Japan is fairly advanced. In other words, the levels are even lower in these countries than in Japan. It is fitting that Japan should work not merely for the solution of its own problems, but at the same time strive for the solution of similar problems in neighboring countries. In the Study Group this point was emphasized particularly by those who had become keenly aware of the conditions in Asian nations through attendance at various international conferences or observation of actual situations in these regions.

In order to assist in solving these problems, it is most desirable that Japan co-operate not only through the specialized agencies which often handle these problems but also through the United Nations itself and particularly through the Economic and Social Council.

*To aid the economi development of underdeveloped regions:* Of all the projects for world peace, one of the most significant is the promotion of the economic development of underdeveloped countries and the elevation of their living standards. Although it may be unspectacular, it is a highly important undertaking. In order to carry out these projects effectively, advanced nations must be active in providing technical assistance and economic co-operation. To leave these activities to one or two powers is likely to invite suspicion or provide material for propaganda that these powers are trying to control the underdeveloped nations by the influence of dollars and pounds. The development of the underdeveloped regions should be carried out through the United Nations with as many member states as possible co-operating in order to make it a truly United Nations project.

From the viewpoint of regionalism, it would be appropriate, as well as effective, for the comparatively industrialized nations within a region to take the initiative in the development of underdeveloped nations in that area. To put it concretely, it is desirable to utilize more fully Japan's scientific, technical, and industrial abilities for the development of the underdeveloped areas in Asia. Of course, the development of the region must be planned for the benefit of the underdeveloped nations themselves. International economic co-operation never lasts nor is it effective unless it is planned in such a way that all the co-operating countries—the donors and the receivers—benefit from it. For Japan, with its industrial capacity, promotion of economic exchange with the raw material zones of Asia is an essential condition for economic independence.

Japan thus possesses a genuine interest in the development of the underdeveloped regions in Asia. Instinctively, Japan regards the subject of economic intercourse with other Asian nations as a matter of life or death. Whatever means might be contrived, if the methods and efforts are identified only with the interests of one nation, it would mean little more than a return to old-fashioned economic nationalism. Having abandoned its past expansionist policy, Japan desires not only that its economic intercourse with Asian nations be of value to itself but also that it be an instrument for the development and economic prosperity of Asia and a contribution to world peace. For such a purpose, it is most desirable that Japan's contribution to the economic development of Asia be coordinated with the projects of the United Nations and that Japan play its role as a member of that Organization. Herein lies the last, but not least, important objective which can be realized through Japan's membership in the United Nations.

# Index

## B



## C

## D

## H



## I

## M



## N

## O



## P

## R



## S

## T

## U

www.ingramcontent.com/pod-product-compliance
Ingram Content Group UK Ltd.
Pitfield, Milton Keynes, MK11 3LW, UK
UKHW020215290926
15470UKWH00001B/199

9 780837 175386